At Issue

Should the
Legal Drinking Age
Be Lowered?

Other Books in the At Issue Series:

At Issue

Should the Legal Drinking Age Be Lowered?

Stefan Kiesbye, Book Editor

GREENHAVEN PRESS
A part of Gale, Cengage Learning

GALE
CENGAGE Learning·

Detroit • New York • San Francisco • New Haven, Conn • Waterville, Maine • London

Elizabeth Des Chenes, *Director, Publishing Solutions*

© 2013 Greenhaven Press, a part of Gale, Cengage Learning

Gale and Greenhaven Press are registered trademarks used herein under license.

For more information, contact:
Greenhaven Press
27500 Drake Rd.
Farmington Hills, MI 48331-3535
Or you can visit our Internet site at gale.cengage.com

For product information and technology assistance, contact us at

Gale Customer Support, 1-800-877-4253
For permission to use material from this text or product, submit all requests online at
www.cengage.com/permissions

Further permissions questions can be emailed to permissionrequest@cengage.com

Articles in Greenhaven Press anthologies are often edited for length to meet page requirements. In addition, original titles of these works are changed to clearly present the main thesis and to explicitly indicate the author's opinion. Every effort is made to ensure that Greenhaven Press accurately reflects the original intent of the authors. Every effort has been made to trace the owners of copyrighted material.

Cover image © Images.com/Corbis.

LIBRARY OF CONGRESS CATALOGING-IN-PUBLICATION DATA

Should the legal drinking age be lowered? / Stefan Kiesbye, book editor.
    p. cm. -- (At issue)
  Includes bibliographical references and index.
  ISBN 978-0-7377-6203-7 (hardcover) -- ISBN 978-0-7377-6204-4 (pbk.)
  1. Teenagers--Alcohol use--United States. 2. Alcoholism--United States. 3. Drinking age--Law and legislation--United States. I. Kiesbye, Stefan.
  HV5135.S57 2012
  363.4'10973--dc23
                                                         2012022095

Printed in the United States of America
1 2 3 4 5 6 7 16 15 14 13 12

Contents

Introduction

The legal drinking age has long been a fiercely debated issue. While many argue that teenagers who are allowed to vote, get married, and serve their country overseas should be allowed to drink alcohol legally, many others point to the decline in drunk-driving fatalities ever since the minimum legal drinking age was set at twenty-one years by the federal government (referred to as MLDA 21), and they warn about the possible dangers of lowering the legal drinking age below this threshold. But aside from the debate, young people continue to binge drink, harming themselves and others, leading some to suggest that a new approach to alcohol is warranted.

Journalist Malcolm Gladwell points out in his February 15, 2010, article in the *The New Yorker* that the debate might be misguided and overlook the real cause for binge drinking and drunk-driving fatalities—our cultural attitude toward alcohol.[1] He writes,

> "The abuse of alcohol has, historically, been thought of as a moral failing. Muslims and Mormons and many kinds of fundamentalist Christians do not drink, because they consider alcohol an invitation to weakness and sin. Around the middle of the last century, alcoholism began to be widely considered a disease: it was recognized that some proportion of the population was genetically susceptible to the effects of drinking. Policymakers, meanwhile, have become increasingly interested in using economic and legal tools to control alcohol-related behavior: that's why the drinking age has been raised from eighteen to twenty-one, why drunk-driving laws have been toughened, and why alcohol is taxed heavily. Today, our approach to the social burden of alcohol is best described as a mixture of all three: we moralize, medicalize, and legalize."

1. Malcolm Gladwell, "Drinking Games," *The New Yorker*, February 15, 2010.

To illustrate his point, Gladwell talks about the Bolivian Camba, "a mestizo people descended from the indigenous Indian populations and Spanish settlers," and about "first- and second-generation Italian-Americans from New Haven," Connecticut, who, in a 1940s study, were asked to keep diaries of their alcohol consumption.

The Camba followed a prescribed weekend ritual. According to Gladwell,

> "The group would sit in a circle. Someone might play the drums or a guitar. A bottle of rum, from one of the sugar refineries in the area, and a small drinking glass were placed on a table. The host stood, filled the glass with rum, and then walked toward someone in the circle. He stood before the 'toastee,' nodded, and raised the glass. The toastee smiled and nodded in return. The host then drank half the glass and handed it to the toastee, who would finish it. The toastee eventually stood, refilled the glass, and repeated the ritual with someone else in the circle. When people got too tired or too drunk, they curled up on the ground and passed out, rejoining the party when they awoke. The Camba did not drink alone. They did not drink on work nights. And they drank only within the structure of this elaborate ritual."

The Italian immigrants in New Haven did not have such a ritual, but for them, alcohol was nothing to get drunk on—it was merely part of the meal, "consumed according to the same quotidian rhythms as pasta or cheese," said Gladwell. They drank with most meals but rarely more than a glass.

From these examples, Gladwell draws the conclusion that, "frat boys drinking in a bar on a Friday night don't have to be loud and rowdy. They are responding to the signals sent by their immediate environment—by the pulsing music, by the crush of people, by the dimmed light, by the countless movies and television shows and general cultural expectations that say that young men in a bar with pulsing music on a Friday night have permission to be loud and rowdy." In short, he suggests, young people learn by example. If society associates alcohol consumption with loud and risky behaviors, such as fights, drunk-driving, and unsafe sex, then teens will act accordingly once they start consuming alcohol. American culture reinforces alcohol as a drug to facilitate loose and reckless behavior, in contrast to the structured alcohol intake of Italians and the Camba.

So why doesn't everyone behave and "drink like the Italians of New Haven?" Gladwell's answer is that "in a perfect world, the rest of us would have adopted the best ways of the [Italian] newcomers. It hasn't worked out that way, though. Americans did not learn to drink like Italians. On the contrary, when researchers followed up on Italian-Americans, they found that by the third and fourth generations they were, increasingly, drinking like everyone else."

Instead of providing teenagers with a positive example of how to drink responsibly, American society, according to Gladwell, only tries to punish or outlaw unwanted behaviors. In his view we are failing every new generation, because we don't have an alternative to irresponsible and reckless behavior when drinking.

Reexamining cultural attitudes around alcohol could be one key to reversing America's trend toward irresponsible drinking and the resulting behaviors. This book offers other opinions, reflecting the varying views on the issue.

1

The Legal Drinking Age Policy Has Been Effective

Substance Abuse Policy Research Program (SAPRP)

The Substance Abuse Policy Research Program is an initiative funded by the Robert Wood Johnson Foundation that focuses on analyzing and informing public and private policies aimed at reducing the harm caused by alcohol, drugs, and tobacco. It also encourages experts in public health, law, political science, medicine, sociology, criminal justice, economics, and psychology to address issues related to substance abuse.

After careful analysis of the available data, more than twenty-five thousand lives have been saved in the thirty years since states began uniformly raising the legal drinking age to twenty-one years. The number of fatal car accidents has significantly decreased, homicides and suicides have been reduced, and binge drinking has not markedly increased. While many people want to see the legal age lowered, European statistics show that alcohol-related problems cannot be avoided by more lenient laws. To the contrary, studies have shown that teenagers form addictive behaviors more easily when introduced to alcohol at a young age and run the risk of sustaining brain damage later in life.

When the age-21 restriction was initiated across states, driver alcohol involvement in fatal traffic crashes declined more significantly among the 18- to 20-year-old population than among drivers aged 21 and older. In 1982, the first year for which alcohol estimates were available in NHTSA's

"Key Results: Mimimim Legal Drinking Age Policy," SAPRP.org, 2009.

[National Highway Traffic Safety Administration] Fatality Analysis Reporting System (FARS), 48% of drivers aged 18 to 20 involved in fatal crashes had some alcohol, compared to 40% for drivers aged 21 and older. In 1989, the year after the last states had enacted their MLDA-21 laws, 34% of drivers aged 18 to 20 involved in fatal crashes had some alcohol, compared to 32% for drivers aged 21 and older. From 1982 to 1989, 18- to 20-year-old drinking drivers in fatal crashes declined 14 percentage points, while drivers aged 21 and older declined by 8 percentage points. In 2006, 26% of the drivers involved in fatal crashes in each age group had some alcohol. Numerous studies since the National Uniform Drinking Age Act have confirmed associations between raising the MLDA to 21 and reductions in underage alcohol consumption, youthful traffic fatalities, and other harm. Research has revealed a decrease in six types of fatal injuries (including deaths related to car crashes, suicides, homicides, falls, drowning, and alcohol poisoning) for 15- to 24-year-olds following implementation of the MLDA-21 law. NHTSA credits state laws raising the legal drinking age to 21 with preventing approximately 900 traffic deaths annually.

Ample Evidence in Support of MLDA 21

A recent study indicated that the laws making it illegal for youth to possess or purchase alcohol if they are younger than age 21 have reduced the rate of underage drinking drivers in fatal crashes by 11%. That analysis controlled or accounted for numerous other factors—other drunk driving laws, alcohol consumption, the economy, the culture of the state, and vehicle miles driven in the state—that could have affected underage drinking and driving. Even with all those factors accounted for, the core laws raising the minimum drinking age to 21 still resulted in a substantial reduction in youth traffic fatalities. This confirms the findings of prior research but has a stronger design than many earlier studies.

NHTSA estimates that minimum drinking age laws have prevented 26,333 traffic deaths since 1975. This estimate represents people of all ages who otherwise would have been involved in a fatal crash involving 18- to 20-year-old alcohol-impaired drivers. This number would be higher if the number of lives saved through the prevention of other underage drinking deaths (e.g. suicides, homicides, unintentional injury deaths) were included.

Researchers have found that as the legal drinking age was lowered, the number of social problems increased, but as the legal age was raised, the number of problems decreased.

Zero-Tolerance Laws Reduce Fatal Traffic Crashes

As of June 1998, all states and the District of Columbia have set a BAC [blood alcohol content] limit of .02 or lower for drivers younger than aged 21 (zero-tolerance law). This law has also been associated with significant reductions in the involvement of drinking drivers aged 20 and younger in fatal traffic crashes. These laws could be made more effective via corresponding media campaigns publicizing them. . . .

Fake identification laws in the states that have criminal or administrative license suspension sanctions account for about a 7% decrease in underage drinking drivers in fatal crashes. States should therefore ensure that these license sanctions are in their laws if they expect it to have an effect on drinking and driving among youths. All 50 states and the District of Columbia have fake identification laws, but only 6 states have administrative license suspension penalties associated with their laws. Eight states do not have any driver's license sanction in their fake identification law.

Reductions in Homicides and Suicides

A review of studies on the effects of minimum age drinking laws on alcohol consumption found that, as the legal age was lowered, drinking increased. Conversely, raising the legal drinking age reduced the consumption of alcohol. Studies show MLDA-21 laws are associated with reductions in homicides, suicides, and unintentional injuries by 18- to 20-year-olds. Alcohol use interacts with conditions such as depression and stress that contribute to suicide, the third leading cause of death among people aged 14 to 25. In one study, 37% of eighth grade females who drank heavily reported attempting suicide, compared with 11% who did not drink. Individuals younger than 21 commit 45% of rapes, 44% of robberies, and 37% of other assaults, and it is estimated that 50% of violent crime involving all ages is alcohol-related. Researchers have found that as the legal drinking age was lowered, the number of social problems increased, but as the legal age was raised, the number of problems decreased. . . .

Those who started drinking at age 18 were nearly twice as likely to be unintentionally injured, be in motor-vehicle crashes, and be in physical fights while under the influence of alcohol compared to those who started at age 21.

Unhelpful Comparisons

Many rights have different ages of initiation. In most states in America, a person can obtain a hunting license at age 12 and drive at age 16. U.S. citizens can vote and serve in the military at 18. Other rights that are regulated include the sale and use of tobacco and the age of legal consent for sexual intercourse and marriage. Vendors, such as car rental facilities and hotels, also have set the minimum age for a person to use their services—25 years old to rent a car and 21 years old to rent a hotel room. The minimum age for initiation is based on the specific behaviors involved and takes into account the dangers and benefits of that behavior at a given age. The minimum age for initiation for certain rights is also based on physical development, including brain function. The military recruits 18-year-olds fresh out of high school because they are physically fit and highly trainable. This does not mean these 18-year-olds are ready for alcohol use, nor would alcohol improve their military performance.

Alcohol affects teens differently than adults. A teenager may look like an adult physically and may even appear more physically fit, but the teenager's body is still developing. It actually takes less alcohol for a teenager to be intoxicated than it does for an adult in his or her twenties. A normal adult's liver can safely process an estimated 50 alcohol calories an hour (one ounce of 40% alcohol). However, studies show that a teenager's liver can only process half that amount. To ingest only 25 alcohol calories per hour, a teenager could drink no more than one-fourth of a "light" beer in one hour. Although adolescence is often characterized by increased independence and a desire for knowledge and exploration, it is also a time when brain changes can result in high-risk behaviors, addiction vulnerability, and mental illness, as different parts of the brain mature at different rates.

The Negative Influence of Alcohol

There is mounting evidence that repeated exposure to alcohol during adolescence leads to long-lasting deficits in cognitive abilities, including learning and memory in humans. In one study of subjects recruited from treatment programs (aged 13 to 19), it was observed that teens who returned to drinking after the treatment program suffered further declines in cognitive abilities, particularly in tests of attention, over the next 4 years.

Early onset of drinking by youth has also been shown to significantly increase the risk of future alcohol-related problems (e.g., alcohol dependence as well as getting into fights, experiencing traffic crashes, and other unintentional injuries after drinking), controlling for a variety of personal demographic characteristics as well as history of smoking and drug use and family history of alcoholism. Further, early drinking onset has been linked to suicide attempts. In addition, the consequences appear to be more severe for those who start drinking at a younger age. In 2004, a joint review for the National Research Council and Institute of Medicine revealed that youth who started drinking before age 15, compared to those who waited until they were 21, were 12 times more likely to be unintentionally injured while under the influence of alcohol, 7 times more likely to be in a motor vehicle crash after drinking, and 10 times more likely to be in a physical fight after drinking. After analytically controlling for history of alcohol dependence, frequency of heavy drinking, years of drinking, age, gender, race/ethnicity, history of cigarette smoking, and illicit drug use, those who started drinking at age 18 were nearly twice as likely to be unintentionally injured, be in motor-vehicle crashes, and be in physical fights while under the influence of alcohol compared to those who started at age 21.

The Danger of Alcoholism

Youth who start drinking at age 18 have twice the odds of drinking to intoxication than youth who start at age 21. Youth who start drinking at age 18 have a 33% to 52% greater chance of being injured while under the influence of alcohol in their lifetime compared to youth who start drinking at age 21. Fifteen percent of youth who start drinking at age 18 become alcohol dependent at some point in their lives compared to only 9% of youth who wait until age 21 before drinking. Youth who started drinking at age 18 have a 2.4-fold increase in risk of being involved in a motor-vehicle crash because of drinking too much in the past year compared to youth who started drinking at age 21. Youth who started drinking at age 18 have a 50% to 60% greater chance of being in a physical fight while drinking or after drinking in the past year compared to youth who started drinking at age 21.

Binge drinking among college students has been fairly steady for the past 10 years.

Research shows that when the drinking age is 21, those younger than 21 drink less and continue to drink less through their early twenties. The lower rates of drinking before age 21 are not compensated for by a higher rate of drinking after reaching 21, as some have conjectured. In fact, research shows that the opposite is true. Early legal access (at age 18) is associated with higher rates of drinking later in life. According to the National Institute on Alcohol Abuse and Alcoholism's (NIAAA's) Initiative on Underage Drinking, 40% of those who started drinking before the age of 15 met criteria for alcohol dependence at some point in their lives. This is four times greater than those who begin drinking at age 21. Twenty-eight percent who start drinking at age 17 and 15% who start drinking at age 18 developed alcohol dependence. Youth who start drinking at age 18 are 1.4 times more likely to become alcohol dependent than those who start at age 21 or older, even after controlling for age, gender, race/ethnicity, education, marital status, family history of alcoholism, childhood depression, antisocial behavior, and history of smoking and drug use. No evidence exists to indicate that young people will learn to drink responsibly simply because they can consume alcohol legally at a younger age. Countries with lower drinking ages suffer from alcohol-related problems similar to or greater than those in the United States.

Lowering the drinking age, as was done in the 1970s in America, has recently been shown to significantly increase alcohol-related traffic injuries for the age groups affected in

New Zealand. Lowering the drinking age from 21 to 18 will also expose more youth to excessive alcohol consumption that can lead to problems with brain function. Ongoing research indicates the brain is not fully developed in many humans until about age 25.

Lower Drinking Ages in Europe

European countries are held up as examples of where more liberal drinking age laws and attitudes may foster more responsible drinking by young people. It is often asserted that alcohol is more integrated into European (especially southern European) culture and that young people there learn to drink at earlier ages within the context of the family. Consequently, young Europeans learn to drink more responsibly than do young Americans. This may be so in a handful of countries, but in reality, a greater percentage of 15-year-olds in most European countries reported being intoxicated in the past 30 days than in the United States. Evidence also indicates that some European youth have higher rates of alcohol-related problems because of their heavy drinking. . . .

Binge Drinking

Binge drinking (i.e., reaching a BAC=.08; typically having five or more drinks for males and four or more for females at a drinking session) is a major problem at many colleges. Binge drinking among college students has been fairly steady for the past 10 years. Between 1997 and 2006, the proportion of college students reporting binge drinking from the Monitoring the Future (MTF) survey ranged from a high of 41.7% in 2004 to a low of 38.5% in 2003. The percentage of college students who reported being drunk in the past 30 days shows similar fluctuations and results between 1991 and 2006, with several ups and downs during that period. Overall, the proportion of 19- to 20-year-olds (college and no college) reporting binge drinking from the MTF survey has fluctuated from a low of 31.7% in 1995 to a high of 37.0% in 1991. The proportion of 12th graders reporting binge drinking in the last 2 weeks from the MTF survey actually declined recently, ranging from 29.8% in 1991 to a high of 31.5% in 1998 to a low of 25.9% in 2007....

There is evidence that communities that combine public information, training for servers, and enforcement of MLDA-21 laws can have an effect on underage drinking by reducing alcohol availability. An evaluation of a multicommunity program entitled Complying with the Minimum Drinking Age (CMDA) demonstrated significant reductions in sales rates to youth due to enforcement checks. Communities Mobilizing for Change on Alcohol (CMCA) have shown evidence of the effectiveness of enforcement programs and efforts in reducing the consequences of underage drinking. A Community Prevention Trial to Reduce Alcohol-Involved Trauma that combined community mobilization, media advocacy, responsible beverage service training, and enforcement showed evidence of reducing sales to underage, underage drinking and driving, and underage injuries.

2

The Legal Drinking Age Has Not Been Effective

Michelle Minton

Michelle Minton is a fellow in consumer policy studies at the Competitive Enterprise Institute, a conservative think tank in Washington, DC. The issues she manages include property insurance, credit unions, gambling industry regulation, and beverage industry regulation. She has appeared as a guest on various radio programs, including the G. Gordon Liddy Show and the Thorn Hartman Show, as well as international television programs. Her work has been published and cited by such national news outlets as the Wall Street Journal *and* USA Today.

Despite drinking ages far lower than twenty-one, European countries have fewer teenage alcohol-related problems than America. The often cited decrease in traffic fatalities since the nationwide introduction of MLDA 21 can be attributed to higher safety standards, law enforcement, and airbags and safety belts rather than to the increase in the legal drinking age. Furthermore, since American teenagers learn to drive many years before they are allowed to drink, they often overestimate their driving ability and have less understanding of how alcohol affects their ability to drive, actually leading to more traffic fatalities. Overall, MLDA 21 has done more harm than good.

Alaska state representative Bob Lynn (R., Anchorage) is asking the long overdue question: Why do we consider 18-year-olds old enough to join the military, to fight and die for our country, but not to have a drink with their friends before they ship out or while they're home on leave? Lynn has introduced a bill [in 2011] that would allow anyone 18 years and older with a military ID to drink alcohol in Alaska.

The bill is already facing strong opposition from self-styled public-health advocates. However, the data indicate that the 21-minimum drinking age has not only done zero good, it may actually have done harm. In addition, an individual legally enjoys nearly all other rights of adulthood upon turning 18—including the rights to vote, get married, and sign contracts. It is time to reduce the drinking age for all Americans.

It's true that America has a problem with drinking: The rates of alcoholism and teenage problem drinking are far greater here than in Europe.

The Historical Background

In the early 1970s, with the passage of the 26th amendment (which lowered the voting age to 18), 29 states lowered their minimum legal drinking age to 18, 19, or 20 years old. Other states already allowed those as young as 18 to buy alcohol, such as Louisiana, New York, and Colorado. However, after some reports showed an increase in teenage traffic fatalities, some advocacy groups pushed for a higher drinking age. They eventually gained passage of the 1984 National Minimum Drinking Age Act, which lets Congress withhold 10 percent of a state's federal highway funds if it sets its minimum legal drinking age below 21. (Alaska would reportedly lose up to $50 million a year if Lynn's bill passes.)

By 1988, all states had raised their drinking age to 21. In the years since, the idea of lowering the drinking age has periodically returned to the public debate, but groups such as Mothers Against Drunk Driving (MADD) have been able to fight back attempts to change the law. (Louisiana briefly lowered its age limit back to 18 in 1996, after the state Supreme Court ruled that the 21 limit was a form of age discrimination, but the court reversed that decision a few months later.)

It's true that America has a problem with drinking: The rates of alcoholism and teenage problem drinking are far greater here than in Europe. Yet in most European countries, the drinking age is far lower than 21. Some, such as Italy, have no drinking age at all. The likely reason for the disparity is the way in which American teens are introduced to alcohol versus their European counterparts. While French or Italian children learn to think of alcohol as part of a meal, American teens learn to drink in the unmonitored environment of a basement or the backwoods with their friends. A 2009 study by the National Institute on Drug Abuse, National Institute of Health, and U.S. Department of Health and Human Services concluded that 72 percent of graduating high-school seniors had already consumed alcohol.

The most likely cause for the decrease in traffic fatalities is a combination of law enforcement, education, and advances in automobile-safety technologies such as airbags and roll cages.

College Binge Drinking

The problem is even worse on college campuses, where there is an unspoken understanding between students, administrators, local law enforcement, and parents that renders drinking-age restrictions effectively moot as students drink alcohol at frat or house parties and in their dorm rooms. The result is dangerous, secret binge drinking. This unspoken agreement and the problems it creates led a group of college chancellors and presidents from around the nation to form the Amethyst Initiative, which proposes a reconsideration of the current drinking age.

Middlebury College president emeritus John M. Mc-Cardell, who is also a charter member of Presidents Against Drunk Driving, came out in favor of lowering the drinking age to 18 years old in a 2004 *New York Times* opinion article. "Our latter-day prohibitionists have driven drinking behind closed doors and underground," he wrote. "Colleges should be given the chance to educate students, who in all other respects are adults, in the appropriate use of alcohol, within campus boundaries and out in the open."

The most powerful argument, at least emotionally, for leaving the drinking age at 21 is that the higher age limit has prevented alcohol-related traffic fatalities. Such fatalities indeed decreased about 33 percent from 1988 to 1998—but the trend is not restricted to the United States. In Germany, for example, where the drinking age is 16, alcohol-related fatalities decreased by 57 percent between 1975 and 1990. The most likely cause for the decrease in traffic fatalities is a combination of law enforcement, education, and advances in automobile-safety technologies such as airbags and roll cages.

Harming Teenagers and Young Adults

In addition, statistics indicate that these fatalities may not even have been prevented but rather *displaced* by three years, and that fatalities might even have increased over the long run because of the reduced drinking age. In an award-winning study in 2010, University of Notre Dame undergraduate Dan Dirscherl found that banning the purchase of alcohol between the ages of 18 and 21 actually *increased* traffic fatalities of those between the ages of 18 and 24 by 3 percent. Dirscherl's findings lend credence to the "experienced drinker" hypothesis, which holds that when people begin driving at 16 and gain confidence for five years before they are legally able to drink, they are more likely to overestimate their driving ability and have less understanding of how alcohol consumption affects their ability to drive.

Statistics aside, the drinking age in the U.S. is difficult to enforce and discriminatory toward adults between 18 and 21 years old. The current age limit has created a culture of hidden drinking and disrespect for the law. Regardless of whether an adult is in the military or a civilian, she ought to be treated as just that: an adult. If you are old and responsible enough to go to war, get married, vote, or sign a contract, then you are old and responsible enough to buy a bottle of beer and toast to living in a country that respects and protects individual rights. It is long past time the law caught up with that reality.

3

Efforts to Lower the Drinking Age Have Both Supporters and Detractors

Radley Balko

Radley Balko is a witer and former policy analyst for the Cato Institute, where he specialized in civil liberties issues. Currently, he is a contributing editor at Reason *magazine and Reason.com.*

Although the United States has had a federal minimum drinking age for over twenty years, the legislation is still as controversial as when it was passed. There is no consensus on whether or not the law has been successful. For example, while supporters cite drops in highway fatalities as proof of success, opponents of the federal minimum drinking age argue this drop is better explained by other factors, such as increased automobile safety regulations. Many citizens also believe that twenty-one is an arbitrary age, when at eighteen one can fight for their country. Passionate arguments from both sides keep the debate on how to safely introduce alcohol to young people ongoing.

It's been 20 years that America has had a minimum federal drinking age. The policy began to gain momentum in the early 1980s, when the increasingly influential Mothers Against Drunk Driving added the federal minimum drinking age to its legislative agenda. By 1984, it had won over a majority of the Congress.

Radley Balko, "Back to 18?: A New Chorus of Critics Say It's Time to Lower the Drinking Age," *Reason*, April 12, 2007. Reason.com. Reproduced by permission.

President Reagan initially opposed the law on federalism grounds but eventually was persuaded by his transportation secretary at the time, now-Sen. Elizabeth Dole.

Legal Drinking Age Legislation Remains Controversial

Over the next three years every state had to choose between adopting the standard or forgoing federal highway funding; most complied. A few held out until the deadline, including Vermont, which fought the law all the way to the U.S. Supreme Court (and lost).

Twenty years later, the drawbacks of the legislation are the same as they were when it was passed.

The first is that the age set by the legislation is basically arbitrary. The U.S. has the highest drinking age in the world (a title it shares with Indonesia, Mongolia, Palau). The vast majority of the rest of the world sets the minimum age at 17 or 16 or has no minimum age at all.

Supporters of the federal minimum argue that the human brain continues developing until at least the age of 21.

Alcohol expert Dr. David Hanson of the State University of New York at Potsdam argues such assertions reek of junk science. They're extrapolated from a study on lab mice, he explains, as well as from a small sample of actual humans already dependent on alcohol or drugs. Neither is enough to make broad proclamations about the entire population.

If the research on brain development is true, the U.S. seems to be the only country to have caught on to it.

Oddly enough, high school students in much of the rest of the developed world—where lower drinking ages and laxer enforcement reign—do considerably better than U.S. students on standardized tests.

Tying Federal Mandates to Highway Funds

The second drawback of the federal drinking age is that it set the stage for tying federal mandates to highway funds, enabling Congress to meddle in all sorts of state and local affairs it has no business attempting to regulate—so long as it can make a tortured argument about highway safety.

Efforts to set national speed limits, seat belt laws, motorcycle helmet laws and set a national blood-alcohol standard for DWI [driving while intoxicated] cases have rested on the premise that the federal government can blackmail the states with threats to cut off funding.

The final drawback is pretty straightforward: It makes little sense that America considers an 18-year-old mature enough to marry, to sign a contract, to vote and to fight and die for his country, but not mature enough to decide whether or not to have a beer.

Effects and Repercussions

So for all of those drawbacks, has the law worked? Supporters seem to think so. Their primary argument is the dramatic drop in the number of alcohol-related traffic fatalities since the minimum age first passed Congress in 1984. They also cite relative drops in the percentage of underage drinkers before and after the law went into effect.

Delaying first exposure to alcohol until young adults are away from home may not be the best way to introduce them to drink.

But a new chorus is emerging to challenge the conventional wisdom. The most vocal of these critics is John McCardell Jr., the former president of Middlebury College in Vermont. McCardell's experience in higher education revealed to him that the federal age simply wasn't working.

It may have negligibly reduced total underage consumption, but those who did consume were much more likely to do so behind closed doors and to drink to excess in the short time they had access to alcohol. McCardell recently started the organization Choose Responsibility, which advocates moving the drinking age back to 18.

The Federal Drinking Age and Highway Fatalities

McCardell explains that the drop in highway fatalities often cited by supporters of the 21 minimum age actually began in the late 1970s, well before the federal drinking age set in.

What's more, McCardell recently explained in an online chat for the *Chronicle of Higher Education,* the drop is better explained by safer and better built cars, increased seat belt use and increasing awareness of the dangers of drunken driving than in a federal standard.

The age at highest risk for an alcohol-related auto fatality is 21, followed by 22 and 23, an indication that delaying first exposure to alcohol until young adults are away from home may not be the best way to introduce them to drink.

After 20 years, perhaps it's time to take a second look.

The Debate Continues

McCardell isn't alone. Kenyon College President S. Georgia Nugent has expressed frustration with the law, particularly in 2005 after the alcohol-related death of a Kenyon student. And former *Time* magazine editor and higher ed reporter Barrett Seaman echoed McCardell's concerns in 2005.

The period since the 21 minimum drinking age took effect has been "marked by a shift from beer to hard liquor," Seaman wrote in *Time*, "consumed not in large social settings, since that was now illegal, but furtively and dangerously in students' residences. In my reporting at colleges around the country, I did not meet any presidents or deans who felt the 21-year age minimum helps their efforts to curb the abuse of alcohol on their campuses."

The federal drinking age has become somewhat sacrosanct among public health activists, who've consistently relied on the accident data to quell debate over the law's merits.

They've moved on to other battles, such as scolding parents for giving their own kids a taste of alcohol before the age of 21 or attacking the alcohol industry for advertising during sporting events or in magazines aimed at adults that are sometimes read by people under the age of 21.

But after 20 years, perhaps it's time to take a second look—a sound, sober (pardon the pun), science-based look—at the law's costs and benefits, as well as the sound philosophical objections to it.

McCardell provides a welcome voice in a debate too often dominated by hysterics. But beyond McCardell, Congress should really consider abandoning the federal minimum altogether, or at least the federal funding blackmail that gives it teeth.

State and local governments are far better at passing laws that reflect the values, morals and habits of their communities.

4

Lowering the Drinking Age: Let's Keep the Dialogue Open

Donald R. Eastman III

Donald R. Eastman III is president of Eckerd College in St. Petersburg, Florida, and one of the signatories to the Amethyst Initiative, an effort consisting of college and university presidents to consider other options, beyond the current policies, to teenage drinking. From 1989 to 1990, Eastman was the executive director of university communications at Cornell University, and from 1991 to 1998, he served as the vice president for university relations at the University of Georgia.

College students, whether or not they are of legal age, consume alcohol. Instead of being allowed to drink responsibly on campus, they often have to drive to bars and clubs, putting themselves and others at great risk. Prohibitive laws do nothing to educate teenagers about the dangers of alcohol consumption and only criminalize their actions. The many alcohol-related deaths of college students show that MLDA 21 alone has not worked well enough to keep young adults safe.

The young Eckerd College student who died four years ago when the car she was riding in ran off I-275 just yards from her exit to the college had been drinking in Tampa bars with her friend who was driving: She was 18; she was headed home to campus; and then she was dead. The friend, also underage, is now serving in prison for DUI manslaughter.

There are a few key points here: First, the 21-year-old drinking age limit did not keep her, as it does not keep most high school and college students, from drinking—if they want to do it. What the current age limit does is make drinking by those younger than 21 an illegal, furtive, clandestine experience, with little to no chance for adult oversight and care. Government surveys have shown that 51 percent of all young people between 18 and 20 are considered binge drinkers, consuming more than four or five drinks during a single occasion. One wonders what role the current age limit plays in that binge-drinking culture.

The 21-year-old drinking age limit arbitrarily divides our community and, much worse, robs us of the chance to create a culture that encourages young people to drink responsibly.

Second, our student was coming home, to us, that night, because she was not legally permitted to drink alcohol on campus. But, as the work done by MADD and others shows, it is not (usually) alcohol that kills, it is drunken driving that kills. It is conceivable that if we had been able to provide a legal and safe environment for responsible drinking on campus, that young woman would be alive today. One of the things we are doing all over this country with our current laws is requiring many of the young men and women under 21 who drink to use automobiles to do so.

Third, Eckerd College is a traditional liberal arts college, which means two things: We are relatively small (most enroll between 1,000 and 2,500 students), and we are very residential (roughly 80 percent of students at such colleges live on campus). Residential liberal arts colleges take the out-of-classroom experience to be just as much a part of an undergraduate's education—and just as much the college's responsibility—as what happens in the classroom. Residential colleges create communities, with faculty and staff deeply involved in the daily lives of their students. Our goal is to teach young adults to think for themselves, with academic and co-curricular programs built upon the best wisdom available about their developmental needs and urging them to make choices that enhance their own, and others', lives.

The solutions to the problems we face need to go far beyond a drinking age limit.

But the 21-year-old drinking age limit arbitrarily divides our community and, much worse, robs us of the chance to create a culture that encourages young people to drink responsibly, if they wish to drink, in a safe environment. What the current law does is send those under 21 who want to drink off campus into a world that takes their money and ignores the rest.

Now I am not absolutely sure lowering the drinking age to 18 will be an unalloyed better deal for my students—maybe it ought to be raised—but I am certain that rethinking this important cultural issue, given all the problems of the current environment, is long overdue. That's all the Amethyst Initiative asks for—to reopen the conversation, a conversation, by the way, that is not simply about alcohol but about good parenting, proactive schools and the development of responsible drinking behaviors in young adults.

The steps we as a society have taken in the past 25 years to address underage drinking are insufficient. A law enforcement system treating underage drinkers as criminals and a federal system that directs funds to highways based on a state's drinking age do little to teach young adults responsible behavior toward alcohol. We shouldn't think that because fewer young adults die from alcohol-related deaths when the drinking age is 21 versus when it was 18 that we have met our responsibilities. Too many young adults, under and over 21, continue to die each year due to alcohol-related deaths. The solutions to the problems we face need to go far beyond a drinking age limit. Since we are so far from perfect now, how can we not reopen a conversation this vital?

5

The Legal Drinking Age May Provide a Safer Environment for Women

Alan Mozes

Alan Mozes is a reporter for HealthDay, *a website and an online organization that specializes in delivering health news to consumers and health-care professionals.*

A new study shows that women who matured when the legal drinking age was twenty-one throughout the United States were less likely to be victims of domestic violence, homicide, and suicide later in life than those who matured when the legal age was eighteen. While the study showed that men are not affected long-term, women who start consuming alcohol at an early age have a notably increased risk of dying from suicide or homicide later in life, or of being the victim of domestic violence.

Entering adulthood in a place and time where the legal drinking age is 18, not 21, seems to put women, but not men, at a long-term higher risk for homicide and suicide, a new study finds.

"We want to make sure people know all of the consequences of the [legal] drinking age," said study lead author Richard Grucza, an assistant professor in the department of psychiatry at Washington University School of Medicine in St. Louis [Missouri]. "Because while the rationale for raising the age was to keep young people from drinking and driving, there wasn't a lot of thought about the long-term habit-formations that may be occurring when young people drink."

Long-Term Risks

Grucza and his colleagues discuss their findings in the February [2012] issue of *Alcoholism: Clinical & Experimental Research*.

In the study, the researchers tracked the histories of Americans who came of age prior to the full implementation of a 1984 federal law establishing 21 as the national drinking age—in other words, people who turned 18 sometime between 1967 and 1989. This was a period when the legal age for drinking still varied widely between states.

The authors noted that in the 1960s and 1970s, many states had *lowered* the minimum drinking age to 18, to reflect parity with eligibility for both the military draft and voting.

However, a subsequent rise in drunk-driving deaths drove many states to revert back to a drinking age of 21—a move later made universal by passage of the 1984 federal law.

Women who had matured when the legal drinking age was below 21 had a 15 percent higher risk of dying from homicide.

In prior short-term analyses, Grucza's team had found that both men *and* women raised in under-21 states engaged in higher rates of alcohol and drug use as adults, and had a higher rate of drunk-driving accidents, homicides and suicides.

In the new study, the authors set out to gauge the longer-term impact of drinking age laws on homicide and suicide, examining data on about 200,000 suicides and 130,000 homicides that took place in the United States between 1990 and 2004.

A Higher Rate of Suicide Attempts

Looking at residents of the 39 states where the drinking age was pushed upward to 21, the team found in 37 of those states that women who grew up being able to drink *below* the age of 21 had a 12 percent higher risk for suicide—a trend that stretched far into adulthood—than women who matured when the legal drinking age was set at 21.

And in 38 out of 39 states, women who had matured when the legal drinking age was below 21 had a 15 percent higher risk of dying from homicide, the study found.

Female victims of homicide are most often killed by an acquaintance, often during episodes of alcohol-fueled domestic violence.

These trends were not mirrored among men, however.

"As for the different findings concerning men and women, it's hard to say why that happened," Grucza said. "We can start by saying that it's well understood that suicide and homicide are very different phenomena for men and women, independent of drinking habits. And perhaps alcohol tips the dynamic. But at this point it's just speculation based on past literature. We don't have the specific data to ferret that out."

There are important gender differences when it comes to suicide and homicide, the researchers pointed out. For example, while women are known to attempt suicide more often than men, men are more apt to carry suicide to completion. So, drinking might raise the number of suicide attempts that end in completion for women, the researchers reasoned.

Domestic Violence

Female victims of homicide are most often killed by an acquaintance, often during episodes of alcohol-fueled domestic violence, Grucza's team noted. Allowing men to begin drinking at a younger age might up the odds of that happening over time, they added.

Regardless, Grucza and his associates concluded that raising the drinking age appears to have had a positive societal impact. They estimate that upward of 600 suicides and 600 homicides have been prevented each year simply by having 21 as the nation's drinking age.

One key to the trend may lie in alcohol's effects on the young brain.

"We suspected that adolescence is a unique period in terms of the brain's response to alcohol and the vulnerability for addiction," Grucza explained. "And, in fact, what we have here is a natural experiment that supports that idea, by demonstrating an unintended but positive consequence that comes from having raised the drinking age."

Dr. James Garbutt, a professor of psychiatry at the University of North Carolina at Chapel Hill, called the study "intriguing."

Public Health Issues

"We've known for some time that changes in the drinking age, initially brought about by efforts to limit drunk driving, has been one of the biggest public health successes in our lifetime," he noted. "But there's been this thought about reducing the drinking age again, because some say, 'College kids are drinking anyways, so why don't we make it legal?'"

"But this is an important finding that shows the evident value of maintaining the 21 drinking age," Garbutt added. "And it is a clear argument that doing so is probably good for public health on multiple levels."

6

The Legal Drinking
Age Helps Prevent
Alcohol-Related Deaths

Darshak Sanghavi

*Educated at Harvard College and Johns Hopkins Medical School,
Darshak Sanghavi worked for several years as a pediatrician for
the US Indian Health Service in Navajo country. Currently, he is
the chief of pediatric cardiology at the University of Massachusetts Medical School and an associate professor. His book,* A Map
of the Child: A Pediatrician's Tour of the Body, *describes a
child's vital organs and how they function.*

*While a number of college presidents have called for reopening
the debate about the legal drinking age, there's no evidence that
more lenient laws abroad curb alcohol consumption and binge
drinking. However, campus control policies and individual states'
law enforcement can heavily influence young adults' alcohol intake. In addition, in states where alcohol advertising is restricted,
college students engage much less in binge drinking. While MLDA
21 needs to be bolstered by stricter law enforcement and heavy
taxation of alcohol to be as effective as it can be, there's no need
to lower the drinking age and put teenagers and college students
at risk.*

L ast week [August 2008], a coalition of presidents from
more than 100 colleges and universities called on authorities to consider lowering the legal drinking age. The so-called

Amethyst Initiative, founded by a fed-up former president of Middlebury College, asserts that "twenty-one is not working" because the current drinking age has led to a "culture of dangerous, clandestine binge-drinking" on college campuses. "How many times," they rhetorically ask, "must we relearn the lessons of prohibition?"

Binge-Drinking Is Soaring

These academic heavyweights—who include the presidents of institutions like Duke [University], Spelman [College], Tufts [University], and Johns Hopkins [University]—believe that lowering the legal drinking age can promote more responsible alcohol use. The familiar argument is that singling out alcohol to make it off-limits is odd, since 18-year-olds may legally join the military, vote, buy cigarettes, and watch porn. Meanwhile over the past decades, binge-drinking has soared among young people. The 1984 federal law that helps determine the legal drinking age is up for renewal next year, and the college presidents believe this law "stifles meaningful debate" and discourages "new ideas" to stop binge-drinking, like allowing kids over 18 to buy alcohol after a course on its "history, culture, law, chemistry, biology, neuroscience as well as exposure to accident victims and individuals in recovery."

> *Those romantic visions of Irish lasses demurely drinking a glass of ale or sophisticated French teens sipping wine just don't reflect reality.*

It's nice to think that simply lowering the drinking age would make college students behave better (as well as cheer loudly). But the Amethyst Initiative—named for the gemstone believed by ancient Greeks to stave off drunkenness—has naively exaggerated the benefits of a lower legal drinking age. They ignore some of the implications of their recommendations, fail to acknowledge their own complicity in the campus drinking problem, and ultimately gloss over better solutions to bingeing. Kind of like addicts might.

A National Experiment

In truth, the higher drinking age saves lives and has little relation to college bingeing. Some history: After her daughter was killed by an intoxicated driver, Candy Lightner founded Mothers Against Drunk Driving and successfully lobbied for the 1984 National Minimum Drinking Age Act (the law that's up for reauthorization in 2009), which gave full federal highway funds only to states that set the minimum age to purchase or consume alcohol at 21 years. Most states immediately complied, setting the stage for a national experiment.

According to the federal study Monitoring the Future, underage drinking dropped instantly. From 1977 to 2007, the percentage of 12th graders drinking at least monthly fell from 70 percent to 45 percent—almost immediately after the law was enacted, and lastingly. Fatal car crashes involving drunk young adults dipped 32 percent, resulting in 1,000 fewer lives lost per year. Impressively, this decrease occurred despite minimal efforts at enforcement; the mere presence of the law was protective. The relationship is likely causal. In 1999, by comparison, New Zealand lowered the drinking age from 20 to 18, and while alcohol-related crashes involving 15- to 19-year-olds subsequently fell, they declined far less than in the overall population. Today, all major public health authorities, including the American Medical Association, Centers for Disease Control, National Highway Traffic Safety Board, and surgeon general, support the higher drinking age.

Permissive Attitudes Don't Work

We also know that kids in more permissive parts of the world don't drink more responsibly. A magisterial 760-page review from the Institute of Medicine in 2004 noted dryly, "As the committee demonstrates in this report, countries with lower drinking ages are not better off than the United States in terms of the harmful consequences of youths' drinking." Those romantic visions of Irish lasses demurely drinking a glass of ale or sophisticated French teens sipping wine just don't reflect reality.

Still, the college presidents signing the Amethyst statement aren't hallucinating about the American version of the problem: There are more binge drinkers on campuses today. Among college students, the percentage of "frequent-heavy" drinkers remained stable from 1977–89, at about 30 percent. However, bingeing began increasing steadily throughout the late 1990s, long after the legal age was increased.

So if we can't blame the drinking age, what's going on? It's key to understand that there are huge disparities in bingeing, depending on where you live and go to school. State bingeing rates vary three- to four-fold, with middle-American states like Michigan, Illinois, and Minnesota far outpacing coastal areas like Washington state, North Carolina, New York, and New Jersey. David Rosenbloom, a professor of public health at Boston University who studies alcohol use, told me bingeing rates at colleges even in the same city can differ dramatically.

Restricting the Promotion of Alcohol

The reasons aren't very complicated: The strongest determinants of college bingeing are weak state and campus alcohol control policies (the regulatory environment) and the presence of lots of bingeing older adults (a locale's overall drinking culture). Impressively, states that severely restrict the promotion of alcohol and its purchase in large quantities—for example, by requiring registration of keg sales, restricting happy hours and beer-pitcher sales, and regulating advertising like billboards—have half the college bingeing rate of states that don't.

In addition to lobbying for these kinds of local laws, college presidents could also promote alcohol education (obviously) and racial and ethnic on-campus diversity (less obviously). As one might expect, alcohol education does help; for example, a brief educational program at the University of Washington reduced long-term binge-drinking in high-risk students. Additionally, young whites drink far more than young African-Americans and Latinos, men drink more than women, and younger students drink more than older students. When mixed, all the groups moderate their alcohol consumption; thus, colleges with greater student diversity have less bingeing across the board.

Of course, in the end a lot of teens will binge-drink, no matter what the law says.

There's a faster and more effective way to reduce underage drinking—and bingeing—as well: Forget the drinking age debate and sharply increase excise taxes on beer, the preferred choice of underage drinkers. (In real dollars, taxes on liquor, and especially beer, have dropped substantially over the past 30 years.) Just as higher cigarette taxes trump all other methods of curbing smoking among young people, higher alcohol taxes stop kids from drinking too much. . . .

Taxation Curbs Bingeing

David Rosenbloom notes that the five states with the highest beer taxes have half the binge drinking of other states. In 2004, the Institute of Medicine concluded, with characteristic understatement, that the "overall weight of the evidence" that higher taxes reduce alcohol abuse and related harm to young adults is "substantial." Just as gasoline taxes today don't fully reflect the societal costs of carbon emissions, alcohol taxes are too low, argue economists P.J. Cook and M.J. Moore, since they cover less than half of alcohol's external costs, including damage done by drunk young drivers.

Of course, in the end a lot of teens will binge-drink, no matter what the law says. But that's not an argument against making the legal age 21 years old to buy and consume it. (After all, a third of high-schoolers have smoked marijuana, and few people want to legalize it for them.) Rather, the current law is best viewed as a palliative medical treatment [relieving symptoms but not curing the disease] for an incurable condition. Chemotherapy can't cure terminal cancer, but it can make patients hurt a little less and perhaps survive a little longer. Similarly, the current drinking age undeniably reduces teen binge-drinking and death a little bit, without any bad side-effects. When there's no complete cure, though, desperate people are vulnerable to the dubious marketing hype of snake-oil peddlers—which is all the Amethyst Initiative is offering up now.

7

The Legal Drinking Age Does Not Prevent Teens from Drinking

Morris E. Chafetz

Morris E. Chafetz, a doctor of psychiatry, founded the National Institute for Alcoholism and Alcohol Abuse in 1970. He was a member of the Presidential Commission on Drunk Driving, director and executive member of the National Commission Against Drunk Driving, and the presidential appointee at the White House Conference for a Drug-Free America. He also established the Health Education Foundation in Washington, DC. Chafetz passed away in October 2011.

Lawmakers need to acknowledge that everyone becomes an adult at age eighteen, and that it is hypocritical to argue that a person is mature enough to vote but not mature enough to have a drink. While there are fewer drunk driving fatalities than before the legal drinking age was raised in the early 1980s, they have decreased at the same rate in countries with lower drinking ages, suggesting that the two events are not related. Plus, there are still many alcohol-related deaths that occur off the highway that MLDA 21 fails to address. Data and statistics have been misinterpreted and turned into junk science for political reasons, in order to push a prohibitionist agenda. States should be allowed to experiment with lowering the drinking age, without having to fear federal penalties.

In 1982 I accepted appointment to the Presidential Commission on Drunk Driving and agreed to chair its Education and Prevention Committee. The Commission met over the next 18 months and ultimately advanced 39 recommendations to President [Ronald] Reagan, in December 1983. All 39 received unanimous Commission approval.

The most conspicuous of those recommendations, and arguably the most controversial, called for raising the minimum legal drinking age to 21 [MLDA 21] nationwide. I will admit to having had serious reservations about this particular proposal. But in the interest of maintaining unanimity, I reluctantly voted yes.

It is the single most regrettable decision of my entire professional career.

The Failure of MLDA 21

Legal Age 21 has not worked. To be sure, drunk driving fatalities are lower now than they were in 1982. But they are lower in all age groups. And they have declined just as much in Canada, where the age is 18 or 19, as they have in the United States.

Young people view 21 as utterly arbitrary—which it is.

It has been argued that "science" convincingly shows a cause-and-effect relationship between the law and the reduction in fatalities. Complicated mathematical formulas, which include subjective estimations (called "imputation") have been devised to demonstrate "proof." But correlation is not cause. We must neither confuse numbers with science nor interpret a lack of numbers as implying an absence of science.

But even if we concede that the law has had some effect on our highways, we cannot overlook its collateral, off-road damage. The National Institute for Alcoholism and Alcohol Abuse, which I founded in 1970, estimates that 5,000 lives are lost to alcohol each year by those under 21. More than 3,000 of those fatalities occur off our roadways. If we are seriously to measure the effects of this law, we cannot limit our focus.

Laws Need to Reflect Reality

And if we broaden our look, we see a serious problem of reckless, goal-oriented, drinking to get drunk. Those at whom the law is directed disobey it routinely. Enforcement is frustratingly difficult and usually forces the behavior deeper underground, into places where life and health are put at ever greater risk. The 600,000 assaults reported annually, the date rapes, the property damage, the emergency room calls do not in general occur in places visible to the public. They are the inevitable result of what happens when laws do not reflect social or cultural reality.

> It is time to liberate ourselves from the tyranny of "experts," who invoke "science" in order to advance a prohibitionist agenda.

The reality is that at age 18 in this country, one is a legal adult. Young people view 21 as utterly arbitrary—which it is. And because the explanation given them is so condescending—that they lack maturity and judgment, these same people who can serve on juries and sign contracts and who turned out in overwhelming numbers to elect our first black president—well, they don't buy it.

And neither do I. And neither should the American public.

Getting Rid of Fake Science

Whether we like it or not, alcohol is woven into the fabric of our world, most of which has determined that the legal drinking age should be 18—or lower. And so far as I can tell, there is no evidence of massive brain impairment, alcohol dependency, or underage alcohol abuse, which the "experts" tell us will be the inevitable result of lowering the age in the United States.

It is time to liberate ourselves from the tyranny of "experts," who invoke "science" in order to advance a prohibitionist agenda. Prohibition does not work. It has never worked. It is not working among 18–20 year-olds now.

The cult of expertise has made parents feel incapable of raising their children. In many states parents are disenfranchised from helping their sons or daughters learn about responsible alcohol consumption. But as a parent and psychiatrist I trust the instinct of parents more than I do the hubris of "experts."

Despite what these latter-day prohibitionists may think, the problem is not the drink—it is the drinker. There should be more emphasis on the person and the surroundings in which alcohol is consumed and less emphasis on alcohol itself. Personal and social responsibility, not the substance, is the real issue.

But so long as the age remains a one-size-fits-all, federally-mandated 21, and so long as any state that may want to try something different, in hopes of reversing the dismal trend of binge-drinking that (maybe or maybe not coincidentally) has become more serious in the years since the drinking age was raised, forfeits 10% of its federal highway funds, nothing is likely to change for the better.

I do not believe that any state should be forced to adjust its drinking age. But I do believe that the genius of federalism should be allowed to work its will unimpeded, and from that genius, not only better practices, but also safer environments and more responsible consumption, are likely to emerge.

8

MLDA 21 Reduces Binge Drinking, with the Exception of College Students

ScienceDaily

ScienceDaily is a science news website. It is updated several times a day with breaking news and feature articles, and covers all fields of the physical, biological, earth, and applied sciences.

Research has shown that binge drinking has declined nationwide since the introduction of the legal drinking age of twenty-one, except for college students. While male students' drinking has remained roughly the same, binge drinking among female collegians has gone up. However, researchers are convinced that lowering the drinking age will not have any positive effects on teenagers' drinking behaviors and view MLDA 21 as a public health success.

New research [2009] from Washington University School of Medicine in St. Louis [Missouri] has found substantial reductions in binge drinking since the national drinking age was set at 21 two decades ago, with one exception: college students. The rates of binge drinking in male collegians remain unchanged, but the rates in female collegians have increased dramatically.

Reporting in the July issue of the *Journal of the American Academy of Child and Adolescent Psychiatry*, the researchers say although policy initiatives aimed at lowering rates of underage drinking generally have been successful and that binge drinking is down among young people overall, it remains a problem on college campuses.

The researchers, led by Richard A. Grucza, Ph.D., assistant professor of psychiatry, analyzed data gathered between 1979 and 2006 by the National Survey on Drug Use and Health. The information comes from more than 500,000 subjects, and the researchers divided them into groups, according to age, sex, ethnicity and student status.

Women Are Drinking More

"We found that overall, binge drinking is less common than it once was," Grucza says. "Young men account for the majority of binge drinkers, and their rates have dropped substantially since 1979. However, at the same time, the 'gender gap' between male and female drinkers has been closing. In this study, we found that women are drinking more, and their rates of binge drinking have risen over the last 30 years."

Binge drinking declined in young men, unless they were in college.

Binge drinking is defined as having five or more drinks on a given occasion. In 2006, the last year for which the data were analyzed, more than half of college-age males, and almost 40 percent of college-age females reported binge drinking. But the researchers found reductions in binge drinking, especially among boys and young men 20 and younger. In males ages 15 to 17, binge-drinking rates declined nearly 50 percent between 1979 and 2006. During the same period, rates declined more than 20 percent in males aged 18 to 20 and 10 percent in males aged 21 to 23.

In women ages 15 to 20 on the other hand, binge drinking was statistically unchanged since 1979. For women 21 to 23, binge drinking rose by about 40 percent.

Meanwhile, binge drinking decreased among men who are African-American, Hispanic or belong to other minority groups. But it increased among minority women.

College Students Are Still Bingeing

The biggest surprises involved differences between college students and men and women of the same age not enrolled in college. Binge drinking declined in young men, unless they were in college. It was up slightly in young women, but significantly higher in college women.

Among 18- to 20-year-old non-college men, binge drinking declined by more than 30% over the study period, whereas it was statistically unchanged among the men in college. For men ages 21 to 23, rates of binge drinking declined just more than 10 percent but remained virtually the same in those of the same age who attended college. In women ages 21 to 23, binge drinking increased about 20 percent among non-students, but the increase was more than 40 percent among women in college.

"The tendency for binge drinking to decline in society has not permeated our college campuses," says Grucza. "Some researchers have speculated that because colleges are made up of young, mostly unmarried people—with no parental control and no spouse to check in with—they may be more likely to drink to excess than people of the same age who live with their parents or have a spouse. Plus, most have easy access to alcohol because at least some of their peers are 21 or older."

High School Students' Access to Alcohol Has Declined

But with the minimum age at 21, Grucza says it's less likely that high school students have peers of legal drinking age.

Since the minimum national drinking age of 21 was signed into law in 1984, it has become more difficult for younger teenagers to get alcohol and apparently has contributed to lower binge drinking rates among those under 18.

He says stable rates of binge drinking among college students and increases in binge drinking among women have offset some of that improvement and developing a better understanding of the reasons for those demographic trends, rather than lowering the drinking age, will assist future efforts to prevent binge drinking.

"Many proponents of lowering the drinking age argue that the higher drinking age has led to more binge drinking," Grucza says. "There is no evidence to support that. Our study and other studies show the higher age has decreased the amount of alcohol consumed by young people, the number of binge-drinking episodes overall, the number of fatal car crashes and other adverse alcohol-related outcomes. There may be good, philosophical arguments about why the drinking age should be lower than 21, but our study demonstrates the higher minimum drinking age has been good for public health."

9

Efforts to Curb College Binge Drinking Spark MLDA Controversy

Shari Roan

Shari Roan has covered health journalism for the Los Angeles Times *for over twenty years. She is the author of three books, including* Our Daughters' Health: Practical and Invaluable Advice for Raising Confident Girls Ages 6–16.

Binge drinking on college campuses nationwide is a growing problem, but health officials and college presidents are divided over what measures to take to keep students safe from the dangers of alcohol consumption, including alcohol poisoning, car accidents, and death. While many studies point out that the legal drinking age has been largely successful, a growing number of college administrators are convinced that MLDA 21 has driven their students to clandestine and more reckless behavior. New measures to curb binge drinking need to be discussed to influence college students' alcohol consumption, and parents' and teachers' oversight, as well as the possibility of lowering the drinking age, should be examined openly and without political prejudice.

Gordie Bailey Jr. had been in college only one month before he overdosed on alcohol. Urged on by members of a frat house he was intent on joining, the 18-year-old drank until he passed out, was dumped onto a couch and was found dead the next morning. The 2004 incident at the University of Colorado was one of the approximately 1,700 alcohol-related deaths that occur among college students each year in the United States. They include traffic accidents, falls, suffocation, drowning and alcohol poisoning. Hundreds of thousands of other students commit crimes, become crime victims, fail classes, make poor sexual decisions or sicken themselves by drinking too much alcohol. In a survey published last year [2007] by the American College Health Assn., just over one-third of college students admitted they had binged on alcohol at least once in the previous two weeks—a number that appears to be rising.

Underage drinking has long alarmed college administrators and health professionals. But now a deep schism is forming among those same people on how to address the problem.

Each side has statistics to support its position—but most of the health and safety evidence falls squarely on the side of an age-21 limit.

Possible Solutions to a Severe Problem

Last month, more than 100 college presidents signed a petition calling for a debate on whether the minimum legal drinking age should be lowered from 21 to 18.

The statement says in part: "Our experience as college and university presidents convinces us that twenty-one is not working. A culture of dangerous, clandestine 'binge-drinking'— often conducted off-campus—has developed."

Some health professionals agree it's time to discuss the proposal, but other health experts and college officials are aghast.

Each side has statistics to support its position—but most of the health and safety evidence falls squarely on the side of an age-21 limit.

"There is a growing body of knowledge that suggests strong reasons for parents and other concerned people to try to keep alcohol out of the hands of young people as long as we can," says Susan Foster, vice president and director of policy research at the National Center on Addiction and Substance Abuse at Columbia University.

Fewer Traffic Deaths

Statistics on traffic fatalities prove the law works, says Michele Simon, research and policy director at the Marin Institute, an alcohol industry watchdog group in San Rafael, Calif. In 1984, a federal standard was established setting the minimum legal drinking age at 21. Since then, traffic fatalities among drivers ages 18 to 20 have fallen by an estimated 13%, according to the National Highway Traffic Safety Administration.

"That is a really important measure of success," says Simon. "Back in the 1970s when states started lowering the drinking age to 18, that's when this experiment began. There were increases in traffic fatalities, and people said let's go back to the way it was. We forget there is so much science and historical context here. We have been down this road before."

For each additional year under age 21 of drinking, the greater the odds he or she would develop alcohol dependence.

Among those studies comparing the years before 1984 with the current era was a 2001 report from the National Institute on Drug Abuse, which found that college students who reported drinking in the last month fell from 82% in 1980 to 67% in 2000.

In 2007, the University of Michigan's annual Monitoring the Future survey found that annual alcohol use by high school seniors has dropped from 77% in 1991 to 66% last year.

Perhaps the strongest evidence for the harmful health effects of drinking at a young age come from studies on biology and addiction, Foster says.

A 2002 report from the American Medical Assn., citing numerous studies, concluded that alcohol use during adolescence and young adulthood causes damage to memory and learning capabilities.

Those on the age-18 side have studies as well.

Alcohol Addiction

A study in the 2006 *Archives of Pediatrics & Adolescent Medicine* found that teens who began drinking before age 14 had a lifetime risk of alcohol dependence of 47% compared with 9% for those who began drinking at 21. For each additional year under age 21 of drinking, the greater the odds he or she would develop alcohol dependence. Though the cause of this correlation is unknown, some experts believe pure biology—priming the young brain to need alcohol—is involved.

"This is a public health problem and a medical problem," Foster says. "It's about the national failure to recognize addiction as a disease. If we think of it as kids behaving badly or breaking the rules, that gets in the way."

And in a 2002 analysis of 33 high-quality studies on the age-21 drinking law's effects, University of Minnesota researcher Traci L. Toomey found that all but one study showed the higher age resulted in lower rates of alcohol consumption and traffic crashes.

"It is the most well-studied alcohol control policy we have in this country," says Toomey, an associate professor in the school of public health. "Usually we find no effect when we do policy studies. Here we have this policy effect that is very consistent—a big chunk of the studies showing this inverse relationship."

Evidence for Change

A growing number of college administrators and health professionals aren't convinced that the age-21 laws help curb problem drinking.

"Not all the evidence is on one side of the question," says John M. McCardell Jr., former president of Middlebury College in Vermont and founder of Choose Responsibility, a nonprofit group that advocates for changes in minimum-drinking-age laws and that circulated the college president's petition. "We're not ignoring science. There is science on both sides of the question."

For example, the reduction in traffic fatalities may be credited to other safety measures, such as the use of restraints, better automobile design, improved hospital trauma care and stricter traffic laws, in addition to the lower drinking age, some studies suggest.

Those on the age-18 side have studies as well.

A 2003 study from the Centers for Disease Control and Prevention found that, though fewer high school-age students drink now compared with the late 1970s, the rates of binge drinking among all adults 18 and older have risen. Published in the *Journal of the American Medical Assn.*, the study encompasses 1993 to 2001 and showed rates of binge drinking have increased the most (56%) among underage drinkers.

A 2003 study showed that in many countries with lower minimum drinking ages, 15- and 16-year-olds are less likely to become intoxicated compared with teens in the U.S.

This out-of-control drinking may be fueled, McCardell says, by the age-21 laws, which drive underage youth to drink in clandestine settings and apart from older adults who might model more appropriate behavior.

"College presidents are limited on campus to a message of abstinence-only," he says. "They can't say drink moderately or drink responsibly. They can only say abstain."

Trends Are Reversing

Though alcohol-related traffic deaths have declined overall since 1982, deaths have begun to inch up again in recent years, according to the National Highway Traffic Safety Administration.

A 2003 study showed that in many countries with lower minimum drinking ages, 15- and 16-year-olds are less likely to become intoxicated compared with teens in the U.S.

It's the way people drink, not the fact of drinking.

McCardell agrees that studies show the younger someone starts drinking, the greater the likelihood of developing alcohol dependence. But, he says, the 2006 *Archives of Pediatrics & Adolescent Medicine* study shows that the correlation is greatest at younger ages.

"Between 13 and 18, the effect is dramatic. But between 18 and 21 it's visible but insignificant," McCardell says. "What we ought to look at is not keeping 18-year-olds from drinking, it's keeping 13-year-olds from drinking."

A major question not answered by research is whether mild or occasional drinking, such as a beer or glass of wine, causes any physical harm or precipitates harmful behavior in 18-year-olds, says Brenda Chabon, associate professor of clinical psychiatry and behavioral sciences at Montefiore Medical Center in New York.

"It's the way people drink, not the fact of drinking," Chabon says. "What would harm a developing brain is repeated hangovers and blackouts and head trauma from falling. But if

someone were drinking moderately from age 18, I haven't seen any data to show that would have harmful effects in the long run."

There is little evidence in humans to suggest that mild to moderate drinking in late adolescence causes any damage, says David J. Hanson, professor emeritus of sociology at the State University of New York at Potsdam, who has studied the literature.

"The research is almost exclusively based on rats and humans who are alcohol addicted," he says. "It doesn't look at moderate drinking at all. We've got a lot of cross-cultural evidence that it isn't harmful at all."

The Role of Parents and Industry

The argument over the minimum legal drinking age has heated up in recent years due to publicity given to out-of-control drinking among college-age youth and tragic deaths such as Gordie Bailey Jr.'s.

"We need to ask what is driving this behavior," Foster notes. "We're really tolerating a culture of substance abuse on our college campuses. There is no evidence that lowering the drinking age would address these problems."

The alcohol industry, which advertises heavily to college students, should come under the microscope, as well as the role of parents in setting attitudes and expectations for their children, she says.

Bailey's stepfather, Michael B. Lanahan, who has started a foundation to raise awareness about college drinking, says he doesn't know if a lower drinking age would have saved his stepson, but he's pleased that the issue is getting attention.

"Parents have to question their own governance of the children in high school," says Lanahan, who lives in Dallas. "Why do so many kids have fake IDs and we let it go? Why do bars get away with serving underage kids? If parents think college presidents are going to police this issue, they are sorely mistaken."

Proposals to curb youth drinking should explore all solutions, not just lowering the drinking age, Toomey says.

"You can't make conclusions without looking at what the research literature says," she says. "McCardell makes these alternative proposals without backing up that they work."

Reopening the Legal Age Debate

Next month, the National Center on Addiction and Substance Abuse at Columbia University will sponsor a conference, "How to Stop Wasting the Best and the Brightest: Substance Abuse at America's Colleges and Universities."

Choose Responsibility's proposal on lowering the drinking age will be open for debate, Foster says. In addition to the petition asking college presidents to consider a lower drinking age, Choose Responsibility proposes that 18-year-olds should be able to consume alcohol with parents and take a course that, upon completion, grants a license to purchase, possess and consume alcohol.

"It's not 1984 any more," McCardell says. "Who can object to examining this closer? We need to do whatever we can as parents, college presidents, responsible citizens to minimize the harm that people do to other people. That is a reasonable goal of public policy."

10

Lowering the Legal Drinking Age Will Not Curb College Binge Drinking

Sara Huffman

Sara Huffman was an editor for ConsumerAffairs.com, as well as a script coordinator for the TV show My Name Is Earl. *She has also directed and produced the documentary* M.I.A., M.D., *which explains the causes of a shortage of primary care doctors in the United States and how it is affecting people.*

Lowering the legal drinking age would only benefit college campuses with low enforcement levels of underage drinking and a high degree of misperception by students of what they consider normal drinking habits. Lowering the MLDA would not benefit other campuses and would most likely have a negative impact on binge drinking.

In 2008, a group of college presidents and chancellors formed the Amethyst Initiative, a call to rethink the current minimum legal drinking age of 21, citing it would cut down on binge-drinking.

They argue that the law encourages underage college students to drink at parties, where binge drinking is common.

Education vs. Prohibition

The main argument states if students as young as 18 could legally drink in bars and restaurants, they might instead learn more-moderate drinking habits, which could then lead to less binge drinking on college campuses.

So far, 135 college presidents have signed the Initiative's public statement urging lawmakers to reconsider the legal drinking age.

But to simply lower the drinking age without an understanding of its effects would constitute a "radical experiment," said Richard A. Scribner, M.D., M.P.H., of the Louisiana State University School of Public Health, one of the researchers on a new study in the January [2011] issue of the *Journal of Studies on Alcohol and Drugs.*

Scribner and his colleagues at BioMedware Corporation in Ann Arbor, MI, along with other institutions found a way to test this "radical experiment" without involving any actual drinking. They used a mathematical model to estimate the effects that a lower drinking age would have on college binge drinking.

The model, based on survey data from students at 32 U.S. colleges, aimed to evaluate the "misperception effect" emphasized by the Amethyst Initiative—that is, the idea that underage students widely perceive "normal" drinking levels to be higher than they actually are and that students would adjust their own habits if they were surrounded by social drinkers rather than binge-drinking party-goers.

Lowering the legal drinking age would be unlikely to curb college binge drinking.

Ambiguous Results

Overall, the researchers found the campuses that were most likely to see a decline in binge drinking from a lowered legal drinking age were those that had the poorest enforcement of underage drinking laws—being surrounded, for instance, by bars that do not check identification—and a significant level of student misperception of "normal" drinking (that is, students thinking that the average fellow student drinks much more than he or she actually does).

If misperception levels were not present or were at the levels shown by the survey data, these campuses would likely see more binge-drinking if the legal age were lowered.

On "drier" campuses, the study found, student misperceptions would have to be even greater.

"The higher the level of enforcement of underage drinking laws, the higher the level of misperception would have to be for the Amethyst Initiative to have any hope of being effective," explained lead researcher Dr. Jawaid W. Rasul, of BioMedware Corporation. "The misperception effect would have to be extremely large."

And without data supporting the existence of such high levels of student misperception, Rasul said, lowering the legal drinking age would be unlikely to curb college binge drinking.

Lowering Legal Age Comes at a Risk

Scribner also pointed out that lowering the drinking age would hot only affect college students but all currently underage young adults.

And past research has suggested that when alcohol becomes more readily accessible to young people, alcohol-related problems, such as drunk driving, go up.

11

Education on Drinking Responsibly Must Replace Neo-Prohibitionism

David J. Hanson

David J. Hanson is professor emeritus of sociology at the State University of New York at Potsdam. He has researched the subject of alcohol and drinking for over forty years and published two books on the topic, Alcohol Education: What We Must Do *and* Preventing Alcohol Abuse: Alcohol, Culture and Control. *Hanson served as alcohol consultant to the Canadian government and has testified before members of the US Congress; his research has repeatedly been reported in the* New York Times *and other major newspapers.*

Prohibition, which was repealed in 1933, has made a comeback by targeting young people, who have historically little economic and political influence. While many legislators claim that restrictive laws concerning underage drinking have been successful in lowering traffic fatalities, the statistical data does not bear out these claims. Furthermore, young people are not deterred by MLDA 21 but use fake identification and commit other illegal acts to drink, or start using other drugs. Just as teenagers learn how to drive, they need to learn how to drink responsibly. Just saying "no" is not enough—teenagers need to learn responsible alcohol consumption.

Underlying minimum age legislation are the assumptions of American prohibitionism: alcohol consumption is undesirable and dangerous; it typically results in problem behavior; and drinking in any degree is equally undesirable because moderate social drinking is the forerunner of chronic inebriation. Naturally, young people, if not everyone, should be protected from alcohol, according to this view. However, following the repeal of the Eighteenth Amendment in 1933, prohibition efforts have largely been age-specific. While repeal abolished Prohibition in general, prohibitionists have tried to maintain their hold over young people. "The youngest age group is . . . chosen as a symbolic gesture because of its political impotence and because . . . there are not major economic consequences. . . ." And there have been no political consequences; young people tend not to vote or otherwise hold politicians accountable for their actions.

Anecdotal statements by students indicated the belief of some that it "might be easier to hide a little pot in my room than a six pack of beer."

MLDA 21 Has Been Largely Ineffectual

Neo-prohibitionists of today typically argue that raising the drinking age to 21 has been beneficial. However, the evidence suggests a different story. For example, a study of a large sample of young people between the ages of 16 and 19 in Massachusetts and New York after Massachusetts raised its drinking age revealed that the average, self-reported daily alcohol consumption in Massachusetts did not decline in comparison with New York. Comparison of college students attending schools in states that had maintained, for a period of at least ten years, a minimum drinking age of 21 with those in states that had similarly maintained minimum drinking ages below 21 revealed few differences in drinking problems. A study of all 50 states and the District of Columbia found "a positive relationship between the purchase age and single-vehicle fatalities." Thus, single-vehicle fatalities were found to be more frequent in those states with high purchase ages.

Comparisons of drinking before and after the passage of raised minimum age legislation have generally revealed little impact upon behavior. For example, a study that examined college students' drinking behavior before and after an increase in the minimum legal drinking age from 18 to 19 in New York State found the law to have no impact on under-age students' consumption rates, intoxication, drinking attitudes or drinking problems. These findings were corroborated by other researchers at a different college in the same state. A similar study at Texas A & M University examined the impact of an increase in consumption or alcohol problems among under-age students. However, there was a significant increase among such students in attendance at events where alcohol was present. There were also significant increases in the frequency of their requests to legal-age students to provide alcohol and in their receipt of illicit alcohol from legal-age students.

The Legal Age Limit Might Increase Drug Use

A longitudinal study of the effect of a one-year increase of the drinking age in the province of Ontario [Canada] found that it had a minimum effect on consumption among 18- and 19-year-old high school students and none among those who drank once a week or more. A similar study was conducted among college students in the State University System of Florida to examine their behavior before and after an increase in the drinking age from 19 to 21. While there was a general trend toward reduced consumption of alcohol after the change in law, alcohol-related problems increased significantly. Surveys at Arizona State University before and after that state raised the legal drinking age from 19 to 21 found no reduction in alcohol consumption. Finally, an examination of East Carolina University students' intentions regarding their behavior following passage of the 21-year-age drinking law revealed that only 6% intended to stop drinking, 70% planned to change their drinking location, 21% expected to use a false or borrowed identification to obtain alcohol and 22% intended to use other drugs. Anecdotal statements by students indicated the belief of some that it "might be easier to hide a little pot in my room than a six pack of beer."

People become responsible by being properly taught, given responsibility, and then held accountable for their actions.

Over the past four decades it has been demonstrated that the proportion of collegiate drinkers increases with age. However, in July of 1987, the minimum purchase age became 21 in all states. Because drinking tends to be highly valued among collegians and because it is now illegal for those under 21 to purchase alcohol, Dr. Ruth Engs and I hypothesized that reactance motivation would be stimulated among such students, leading more of them to drink. The data from 3,375 students at 56 colleges across the country revealed that, after the legislation, significantly more under-age students drank compared to those of legal age. Thus, the increase in purchase age appears to have been not only ineffective but actually counterproductive, at least in the short run.

Promoting Healthy Drinking

The prohibitionists and their current neo-prohibitionists counterparts are clearly wrong in their assumptions. Drinking in moderation is neither undesirable nor dangerous but is actually associated with better health and greater longevity than is either abstention or heavy drinking. In short it is not bad but good and healthful. And drinking does not typically result in problem behavior. Similarly, moderate drinking is clearly not a forerunner of inebriation. To the contrary, the vast majority of drinkers enjoy the benefits of alcohol and never become problem drinkers.

People become responsible by being properly taught, given responsibility, and then held accountable for their actions. We don't tell young people to "just say no" to driving, fail to teach them to drive, and then on their 18th birthday give them drivers licenses and turn them loose on the road. But this is the logic we follow for beverage alcohol because neo-prohibitionism underlies our alcohol policy.

It's time for our alcohol policy to be based on science rather than ideology.

12

States Should Be Allowed to Experiment with the Legal Drinking Age

John Richards

John Richards is a writer for LegalMatch.com and the Legal Match.com Law Blog.

Serious doubts have been raised about the overall effectiveness of the legal drinking age, but politicians are reluctant to raise the polarizing issue out of fear that it may impact their reelection. As of now, the data gathered about the MLDA's impact are not conclusive, but states should be able to lower the drinking age without being penalized by the federal government. The problem of drinking and drunk driving will not be solved until states are free to experiment with alternatives to the MLDA.

For just about all people under the age of 30, we've never known a time when the legal drinking age was under 21. Or, the legal drinking age went up to 21 (from 18, in most states) long before it would have made any difference to us.

However, in most countries around the world, and for much of America's history (starting when strict enforcement of legal drinking ages began), the drinking age is/was 18.

However, beginning in the mid-1980s, states began to raise their legal drinking ages to 21, en masse. By 1988, every state which had previously had a lower drinking age, had raised it to 21. What happened?

Fighting Drunk Driving

Well, beginning in the 1980s, people began to take the problem of drunk driving seriously. A group known as "Mothers Against Drunk Driving" was founded in 1980, and quickly became the most vocal and visible proponent of strong measures to reduce drunk driving.

This led to Congress passing a law in 1984, which withheld some highway funds from any state that did not raise its legal drinking age to 21. By 1986, almost every state had acquiesced. The last state to do so, Wyoming, held out until 1988. Every state found that it simply could not maintain its roads without the federal money.

I'm not entirely sure why Congress didn't simply mandate a national drinking age of 21. It's possible that some members of Congress thought that the federal government wouldn't have the constitutional authority to do so, or maybe it was simply to give states the illusion of choice.

In any case, the de facto national drinking age has been 21 for over 20 years now.

After all, who is going to vote against the pleas of a mother who lost a child to a drunk driver?

And because I'm writing a blog post on the subject, you've probably guessed that the intended effects of this law have not exactly panned out, and have arguably made things worse. Some studies suggest that, by eliminating legal access to alcohol for people aged 18–20 (when many young adults begin drinking, anyway), drinking by this age group has been driven out of bars and restaurants, and into frat houses and dorm rooms. This means there is less supervision by non-intoxicated people, and nobody encouraging moderation.

Old Enough to Fight

Taking notice of this fact, a law professor and an organization of 130 college presidents have called for the 1984 law to be repealed, effectively placing the question of the appropriate drinking age back into the hands of the states. Reflecting the "old enough to fight, old enough to drink" argument, one Alaska politician has suggested lowering the drinking age to 18 for active duty military personnel.

Personally, I think that this would be a good start, but I see no reason why the drinking age for everyone couldn't be lowered to 18, *assuming that these factual assertions are correct.* While I believe that drunk driving is a problem, and don't doubt that more drunken driving accidents involve young adults than other age groups, that's no reason to retain a law that's ineffective, or at the very least, engage in a serious examination of its effectiveness.

However, it seems that certain laws, regardless of their actual effectiveness (or lack thereof) are viewed as sacrosanct [untouchable] by politicians. After all, who is going to vote against the pleas of a mother who lost a child to a drunk driver?

These days, it seems as if every politician is perpetually running for re-election, so they seem more interested in taking actions that will make good campaign ad sound bytes, rather than enacting policies which they believe to be right.

And I should note that I'm not 100% sure that the factual assertions (that raising the drinking age has done little to combat drunk driving, and increased rates of unhealthy drinking behavior) are correct. There seem to be conflicting studies on the subject. My point is more that we need to honestly examine whether or not laws like this are effective.

Letting States Decide

And if we find that these laws are ineffective, and may actually increase unsafe and unhealthy drinking behavior (binge drinking, drinking without any sober people present, etc.), we should consider different measures that might work.

Furthermore, placing the matter of the legal drinking age back into the hands of individual states would essentially create 50 "policy laboratories," in which different approaches to the problem of drunk driving could be experimented with more freely, including (but certainly not limited to) adjusting the drinking age. And, if one state comes up with a policy that actually lowers the rates of drunk driving, without increasing rates of "underground" binge drinking, then other states would be able to emulate it.

13

Differences in Drinking Cultures Between US and European Youth Are Subtle

Christopher Sopher

Christopher Sopher is a journalism consultant at the John S. and James L. Knight Foundation, as well as a writer for Younger Thinking, a website devoted to publishing ideas and news about young people, and dissemenating a younger perspective on issues and events.

While many Americans still believe that Europeans deal with alcohol use in a more relaxed and sophisticated manner, current globalization has closed the gap between the cultures, with binge drinking on the rise throughout the European Union. Statistics show that a lower drinking age may result in younger binge drinkers. However, since many Europeans are allowed to drink legally at age sixteen, there is no incentive for them to binge drink in secret or to celebrate excessively once they reach the legal age.

Many Americans idolize a culture where Europeans—accustomed to alcohol after years of experience in their teenage years—supposedly know how to avoid binge drinking, alcohol poisoning and hazy nights of bad judgment. It's a particularly popular topic of conversation among 19-year-old college students, waiting in grocery store parking lots for older friends to bring out cases of beer. "The drinking age is so stupid," they say. "If only it was like it is in Europe," suggesting with little sense of irony that, were the drinking age lower, they would both drink more moderately and enjoy the new found freedom to buy $11 cases of Natural Light.

Gaining Experience

In theory, it's a winning idea for all involved. Young people can drink earlier in their lives, which promises more of the freedom from judgment and reason teenagers desire. Parents can believe their children are getting important early experience that, as in any other sport, helps them become better players—and helps them get a head start on the 10,000 hours of practice Malcolm Gladwell [American writer and journalist] says are necessary to become an expert at something. And the data shows many European and American young people are already well on their way.

Binge drinking culture is definitely growing in Europe, and alcoholism has always been a problem.

But the evidence also suggests the differences between how young people drink in Europe and the United States aren't nearly as great as we imagine—and the generational changes are tremendous. By most measures, European youth actually drink more, get drunk more, and do so earlier in life than their American peers (though in certain settings, such as colleges and universities, American youth still lead the drinking world). And there's surprisingly little evidence that introducing young people to alcohol earlier or lowering the drinking age does anything except lower the age at which young people start to drink.

"The number of British, German, Scandinavian and other teenagers stumbling into hostels at 5 a.m. in London, Paris or Prague is pretty overwhelming," said one American college student traveling in Europe, who asked not to be named discussing drinking. "Lax drinking laws, a low drinking age, and a plethora of discos, bars and clubs give kids a lot of opportunities to get totally out of control."

Binge Drinking Is on the Rise

Survey data and the concern of European officials support her observation. A 2008 survey found that "while young people in most European countries are drinking less frequently than their parents and grandparents, they are consuming more alcohol each time they drink," which is similar to the U.S. trend of infrequent but heavy drinking. Data from major surveys compiled by the U.S. Department of Justice found that the U.S. had lower rates of drinking and binge drinking among 15–16-year-olds than every European country except Turkey (which, as a predominantly Muslim country, has strong cultural stigmas against alcohol).

The evidence suggests that the differences in drinking culture between American and European youth aren't as tremendous as we often assume.

"Drinking to get drunk" has become much more common in Europe over the past two decades, with several surveys reporting a growing number of teenagers and young adults who say they drink for the "buzz" or to "get [insert your favorite term for drunkenness]."

"Binge drinking culture is definitely growing in Europe, and alcoholism has always been a problem," said Charles Pellegrin, a French graduate student who has lived in several countries.

Traditionally beer-oriented countries such as the UK [United Kingdom], Ireland, Denmark and Germany lead the statistics on youth drinking, drunkenness and alcohol-related problems—but wine countries appear to be catching up as

French, Spanish and Italian young people choose beer and liquor over wine, and choose it in larger quantities.

Several Spanish and American students I interviewed discussed the trend of "botellon," (literally "big bottle") where Spanish teenagers sit outside in parks or on the street and drink together. This summer France has been overrun by the phenomenon called "apéro géant" ("giant aperitif"), where thousands of young people gather in flashmobs in French cities to party and drink very, very heavily.

The Myth of Early Familiarization

All of this suggests that the merits of a lower drinking age and of early familiarization with alcohol might be something of a myth, too. In many European countries, the discussion about binge drinking is focused on 13-, 14- and 15-year-olds, not college students. Many European authorities are encouraging parents to take a more active role in educating their children about, and discouraging them from, drinking.

"I think that a lower drinking age just causes binge drinking a little earlier," said one American student who studied abroad in Spain.

The evidence suggests that the differences in drinking culture between American and European youth aren't as tremendous as we often assume. And in a globalized world where you can buy a Bacardi Breezer in 30 languages, that isn't surprising. The differences seem more subtle, more cultural.

"Much like in the U.S., there are parties that result in people being a little too drunk," said the American living in Switzerland. "I think that is the same across the globe, but here in Europe, alcohol is less frowned upon. But I can say for sure, when kids celebrate their sixteenth or eighteenth birthday over here, there is no focus of, 'Yes! Now we can drink!'"

14

The Globalization of Culture Influences Young Drinkers

Peter Allen

Peter Allen is a journalist and author based in Paris. He contributes to a wide range of British national newspapers and magazines, and specializes in French current affairs.

The image of France as a country of sophisticated drinkers is slowly crumbling, thanks to a youth culture focused on imitating their Anglo-Saxon counterparts. Binge drinking—once thought to be the territory of British or American teens—has swept up French youth, and in the process the country has become the fourth-largest consumer of alcohol in Europe. Binge drinking is seen as an expression of the globalization of youth culture, led by images from Hollywood and reality TV.

Midnight on the Left Bank [Paris, France] and the cafes and bars on Place St-Michel are, on the surface at least, unchanged from the 1920s, when Ernest Hemingway immortalised one in the opening chapter of *A Moveable Feast*.

Rather than an uncharacteristically restrained American author gorging himself on oysters, rum and white wine, however, the scene early yesterday morning [July 2011] was more reminiscent of a British town centre at closing time. The air was thick with confrontations, arguments and expletives. Welcome to late-night drinking culture, Paris-style.

Being Boisterous Is Cool

"The French kids are the worst because they want to be Anglo-Saxons," said Jean-Christophe, a waiter, shaking his head in front of the Saint Michel archangel fountain, which dominates the square and is currently full of white bath foam and at least one mooning reveller.

"They start knocking back the strong beers early on and then move on to shots, often without eating," Jean-Christophe said, as if describing a sacrilegious act. "They know it's what the English do, and they think it's cool to be boisterous. The kids become so intoxicated that they vomit and urinate anywhere they can find, and they'll be up for a fight too. Pretty soon you have disturbances all over the area, and that's when the police arrive. It's not something we're used to in Paris, and everything needs to be done to control it."

Gendarmes circle in white vans, often supported by units from the CRS (Compagnies Républicaines de Sécuritée), who made their name quelling riots during more idealistic days on the Left Bank, most notably spring 1968. The "flics" look as menacing as ever, complete with body armour, truncheons [clubs] and pistols, even though they are mostly dealing with shambolically [chaotically] intoxicated youths rather than would-be revolutionaries.

As recently as the early 2000s, the French largely viewed drinking to excess as something associated with pot-bellied British visitors.

At some €7 (£6.20) for a pint of lager in cafes such as Le Départ and La Fontaine, it is unsurprising that the worst behaviour comes from those who buy their alcohol at all-night convenience stores. To combat the problem, some cities, including Lyon, have introduced a 10pm to 6am ban on retail sales of beer, wine and spirits. Those who break the embargo face fines of up to €750 (£660).

Introducing Bans on Public Drinking

Maxime Bono, the mayor of La Rochelle on the Atlantic coast, has also banned drinking in public areas, saying: "It's with a heavy heart that I've followed the example of other towns. La Rochelle won't stop being a place where people have fun, but we have to correct some excesses."

Officials at Paris city hall acknowledge that the introduction of such measures is inevitable if they are to halt the "massive and brutal" summer consumption of alcohol in public, and associated nuisances including "damage, violence, noise and the breaking of glass". Individual arrondissements [municipal districts in Paris], including the fashionable 11th, have already introduced occasional bans on drinking in public, and many more are expected.

As recently as the early 2000s, the French largely viewed drinking to excess as something associated with pot-bellied British visitors, often ones wearing replica football shirts or mini skirts, even in the depths of winter. But now even the Académie Française—just a short stroll along the Seine from Place St-Michel—has offered no objection to the term "le binge drinking" being applied to the French citizens whose language it seeks to regulate (the term is actually less of a mouthful than "intoxication alcoolique aigue"—its best Gallic translation).

> *I was often shocked to see talented students rolling about following a night of over-indulgence, but that's exactly what's happening over here now.*

"It's an expression which is becoming increasingly prevalent across France," said Nabila Ramdani, a Parisienne commentator on Anglo-French affairs who was used to seeing the worst effects of excessive drinking during her time as a lecturer at Oxford University [in the United Kingdom].

Imitating Excessive Behavior

"Colleges bridged the class divide when it came to British undergraduates getting drunk, and young people in France are now following suit," she said.

"I was often shocked to see talented students rolling about following a night of over-indulgence, but that's exactly what's happening over here now. It's to do with an increasing rejection of traditional French life, especially by young people."

She added: "Whereas once they would enjoy a glass of wine at family dinners, and drink coffee in cafes, [now] they see the excesses of their counterparts across the Channel as something to emulate. Alcohol is associated with a glamorous, exciting life, and the chance to express yourself."

Dr Georges Picherot, of Nantes University Hospital, western France, told the newspaper *Liberation* he was used to treating children as young as 10 found drunk in the middle of the afternoon. He said the problem was initially viewed as "something festive", but was becoming far more sinister, causing depression, sexual violence and, in extreme cases, death.

Public Mayhem via Facebook

Last month a giant apéro—officially a pre-dinner drink—organised on Facebook in Nantes, attracted 6,000 young people and led to widespread problems, including drunks falling into the Loire River and having to be rescued.

Picherot said he was particularly worried about the increase in drinking within the 18-to-25 age group, especially among young women, many of whom see getting drunk as quickly as possible as being fashionable.

"It's fun and it allows us to let off steam," said Claudine, a 20-year-old Sorbonne University student who was drinking pints of Guinness in Corcoran's, an Irish pub just off Place St-Michel, on Friday night.

"A few years ago the French, let alone French women, would never have dreamed of using pint glasses, but times have changed," she said. "Many of us see our futures in Anglo-Saxon countries like Britain and America, because France is too old-fashioned.

"We know it is very hard to socialise and succeed in countries like these unless you know how to drink. If enjoyed sensibly, alcohol is fine—it makes us feel happy, and it certainly helps to break down barriers between people."

A World Health Organisation report last year showed France to be the fourth largest consumer of alcohol in Europe, after Estonia, the Czech Republic and Ireland.

Taking Risks in Life

Jerome, a 24-year-old maths student at the Sorbonne, said: "There are too many people who want to turn towns like Paris into a ghost town, with alcohol and noise banned. This isn't how modern cities operate. We can easily look up the dangers of drinking on the internet, but you have to take some risks in life."

A World Health Organisation report last year showed France to be the fourth largest consumer of alcohol in Europe, after Estonia, the Czech Republic and Ireland. Britain was in a relatively low 13th position. While such statistics can be misleading (moderate but widespread wine consumption among France's adult population pushes figures up), alcohol remains the third biggest cause of avoidable Gallic deaths. Research by INPES, the national institute for health education, suggests alcohol is responsible for 45,000 deaths in France every year—23,000 for which it is directly responsible, and 22,000 indirectly.

Campaigners pushing for the Lyon and La Rochelle-style bans to be extended point to the fact that half of all domestic violence in France, and a third of all custodial sentences, are attributed to alcohol. But it is the increasingly debauched night-time scenes around national landmarks like Place St-Michel, which is less than two miles from the Elysée Palace, which will inevitably lead to more regulation.

The Global Trend of Binge Drinking

"It's not surprising that the French use a British expression for binge drinking because they believe it's an imported problem," said Ms Ramdani.

"It's associated with irreverent, coarse societies rather than ones in which everybody is treated with dignity and respect. The problem is that such values are becoming less relevant, especially within the 'look-at-me' culture of reality TV, celebrity magazines and Hollywood. Binge drinking fits into a modern, global culture, and that's why, in the long term, France is going to have trouble keeping it in check."

Organizations to Contact

The editors have compiled the following list of organizations concerned with the issues debated in this book. The descriptions are derived from materials provided by the organizations. All have publications or information available for interested readers. The list was compiled on the date of publication of the present volume; names, addresses, phone and fax numbers, and e-mail and Internet addresses may change. Be aware that many organizations take several weeks or longer to respond to inquiries, so allow as much time as possible.

Al-Anon Family Group Headquarters
1600 Corporate Landing Pkwy., Virginia Beach, VA   23454
(757) 563-1600 • fax: (757) 563-1655
website: www.al-anon.alateen.org

Al-Anon Family Groups is a fellowship of men, women, and children whose lives have been affected by an alcoholic family member or friend. Members share their experiences, strength, and hope to help each other and perhaps to aid in the recovery of the alcoholic. Al-Anon Family Group Headquarters provides information on its local chapters and on its affiliated organization, Alateen. Its publications include the monthly magazine the *Forum*, the semiannual *Al-Anon Speaks Out*, the bimonthly *Alateen Talk*, and several books, including *How Al-Anon Works for Families & Friends of Alcoholics, Paths to Recovery: Al-Anon's Steps, Traditions, and Concepts*, and *Courage to Be Me: Living with Alcoholism*.

Alcoholics Anonymous (AA)
General Service Office, PO Box 459
Grand Central Station, New York, NY   10163
(212) 870-3400 • fax: (212) 870-3003
website: www.aa.org

Alcoholics Anonymous (AA) is an international fellowship of people who are recovering from alcoholism. Because AA's primary goal is to help alcoholics remain sober, it does not sponsor research or engage in education about alcoholism. AA does, however, publish a catalog of literature concerning the organization as well as several pamphlets, including *Is AA for You?*, *Young People and AA*, and *A Brief Guide to Alcoholics Anonymous*.

American Society of Addiction Medicine (ASAM)

4601 N Park Ave., Upper Arcade No. 101
Chevy Chase, MD   20815
(301) 656-3920 • fax: (301) 656-3815
e-mail: email@asam.org
website: www.asam.org

ASAM is the nation's addiction medicine specialty society dedicated to educating physicians and improving the treatment of individuals suffering from alcoholism and other addictions. In addition, the organization promotes research and prevention of addiction and works for the establishment of addiction medicine as a specialty recognized by the American Board of Medical Specialties. The organization publishes medical texts and a bimonthly newsletter.

Canadian Centre on Substance Abuse/Centre canadiene de lutte contre l'alcoolisme et les toxicomanies (CCSA/CCLAT)

75 Albert St., Suite 300, Ottawa   ON KIP 5E7
   Canada
(800) 244-4788 • fax: (613) 235-8101
website: www.ccsa.ca

A Canadian clearinghouse on substance abuse, the CCSA/CCLAT works to disseminate information on the nature, extent, and consequences of substance abuse and to support and assist organizations involved in substance abuse treatment, prevention, and educational programming. The CCSA/CCLAT publishes several books, including *Canadian Profile: Alcohol, Tobacco, and Other Drugs*, as well as reports, policy documents, brochures, research papers, and the newsletter *Action News*.

Center for Substance Abuse Prevention (CSAP)
and the National Clearinghouse for Alcohol and
Drug Information (NCADI)
PO Box 2345, Rockville, MD   20847-2345
(800) 729-6686
website: www.samhsa.gov

Both CSAP and NCADI are agencies within the federal government's Substance Abuse and Mental Health Services Administration. CSAP leads US government efforts to prevent alcoholism and other drug problems among Americans. Through the NCADI, CSAP provides the public with a wide variety of information on alcoholism and other addictions. Its publications include the bimonthly *Prevention Pipeline*; the fact sheet *Alcohol Alert*; monographs such as *Social Marketing/Media Advocacy* and *Advertising and Alcohol*; and brochures, pamphlets, videotapes, and posters. Publications in Spanish are also available at its website.

Centre for Addiction and Mental Health (CAMH)
33 Russell St., Toronto, ON   M5S 2S1
  Canada
(416) 535-8501
website: www.camh.net

CAMH is a public hospital and the largest addiction facility in Canada. It also functions as a research facility, an education and training center, and a community-based organization providing health and addiction prevention services throughout Ontario, Canada. Further, CAMH is a Pan American Health Organization and World Health Organization Collaborating Centre. CAMH publishes the quarterly *CrossCurrents* and the *Journal of Addiction and Mental Health*, and offers free alcoholism prevention literature that can either be downloaded or ordered on its website.

Distilled Spirits Council of the United States (DISCUS)
1250 I St. NW, Suite 900, Washington, DC   20005
(202) 628-3544
website: www.discus.org

The Distilled Spirits Council of the United States is the national trade association representing producers and marketers of distilled spirits in America. It seeks to ensure the responsible advertising and marketing of distilled spirits to adult consumers and to prevent such advertising and marketing from targeting individuals below the legal purchase age. DISCUS publishes fact sheets, the periodic newsletter *News Release,* and several pamphlets, including the *Drunk Driving Prevention Act.*

International Center for Alcohol Policies (ICAP)

1519 New Hampshire Ave. NW, Washington, DC   20036
(202) 986-1159 • fax: (202) 986-2080
website: www.icap.org

The International Center for Alcohol Policies is a nonprofit organization dedicated to helping reduce the abuse of alcohol worldwide and to promote understanding of the role of alcohol in society through dialogue and partnerships involving the beverage industry, the public health community, and others interested in alcohol policy. ICAP is supported by eleven major international beverage alcohol companies. The center publishes reports on pertinent issues of alcohol consumption, such as *Safe Alcohol Consumption, The Limits of Binge Drinking, Health Warning Labels, Drinking Age Limits, What Is a "Standard Drink"?, Government Policies on Alcohol and Pregnancy, Estimating Costs Associated with Alcohol Abuse,* and *Who Are the Abstainers?*

Mothers Against Drunk Driving (MADD)

511 E John Carpenter Fwy., No. 700, Irving, TX   75062
(800) GET-MADD • fax: (972) 869-2206
e-mail: info@madd.org
website: www.madd.org

Mothers Against Drunk Driving seeks to act as the voice of victims of drunk driving accidents by speaking on their behalf to commnities, businesses, and educational groups, and by providing materials for use in medical facilities and health and driver education programs. MADD publishes the biannual *MADDvocate for Victims Magazine* and the newsletter *MADD in Action*, as well as a variety of brochures and other materials on drunk driving.

**National Council on Alcoholism
and Drug Dependence (NCADD)**
12 W 21st St., New York, NY   10010
(212) 206-6770 • fax: (212) 645-1690
website: www.ncadd.org

NCADD is a volunteer health organization that helps individuals overcome addictions, advises the federal government on drug and alcohol policies, and develops substance abuse prevention and education programs for youth. It publishes fact sheets, such as *Youth and Alcohol,* and pamphlets, such as *Who's Got the Power? You . . . or Drugs?* which are available on its website.

**National Institute on Alcohol Abuse
and Alcoholism (NIAAA)**
6000 Executive Blvd., Wilco Building
Bethesda, MD   20892-7003
website: www.niaaa.nih.gov

The National Institute on Alcohol Abuse and Alcoholism is one of the eighteen institutes that comprise the National Institutes of Health. NIAAA provides leadership in the national effort to reduce alcohol-related problems. NIAAA is an excellent source of information and publishes the quarterly bulletin, *Alcohol Alert*; a quarterly scientific journal, *Alcohol Research and Health*; and many pamphlets, brochures, and posters dealing with alcohol abuse and alcoholism. All of these publications, including NIAAA's congressional testimony, are available on its website.

Secular Organizations for Sobriety (SOS)
PO Box 5, Buffalo, NY   14215
(716) 834-2922
website: www.sossobriety.org

SOS is a network of groups dedicated to helping individuals achieve and maintain sobriety. The organization believes that alcoholics can best recover by rationally choosing to make sobriety rather than alcohol a priority. Most members of SOS reject the spiritual basis of Alcoholics Anonymous and other similar self-help groups. SOS publishes the quarterly *SOS International Newsletter* and distributes the books *Unloaded: Staying Sober and Drug Free* and *How to Stay Sober: Recovery Without Religion*, written by SOS founder James Christopher.

Bibliography

Books

David Brown

Drunk Driving, Athlete Career Killer: Say NO! to Drinking and Driving. Niles, OH: Parkway Press, 2010.

Donna Cornett

Beat Binge Drinking: A Smart Drinking Guide for Teens, College Students and Young Adults Who Choose to Drink. Santa Rosa, CA: People Friendly Books, 2011.

William Crano and Radmila Prislin, eds.

Attitudes and Attitude Change. New York: Psychology Press, 2010.

Amitava Dasgupta

The Science of Drinking: How Alcohol Affects Your Body and Mind. New York: Rowman & Littlefield Publishers, 2011.

Barrie Gunter

Alcohol Advertising and Young People's Drinking: Representation, Reception and Regulation. New York: Palgrave Macmillan, 2010.

Margaretha Jarvinen and Robin Room

Youth Drinking Cultures. London, United Kingdom: Ashgate, 2007.

Lloyd Johnston et al.

Monitoring the Future: National Results on Adolescent Drug Use, Overview of Key Findings, 2010. Ann Arbor, MI: Institute for Social Research, University of Michigan, 2011.

Barron Lerner

One for the Road: Drunk Driving Since 1900. Baltimore, MD: The Johns Hopkins University Press, 2011.

Bob Mitchell

Drunk Driving and Why the Carnage Continues. Bloomington, IN: Xlibris Corporation, 2010.

Garrett Peck

The Prohibition Hangover: Alcohol in America from Demon Rum to Cult Cabernet. Piscataway, NJ: Rutgers University Press, 2009.

Andrew Percy and Dorota Iwaniec

Teenage Drinking: Causes and Consequences. Saarbrücken, Germany: Lambert Academic Publishing, 2010.

Debbie Shooter and William Shooter

Drugs and Alcohol 101. Orlando, FL: Off Campus Education and Publishing, 2010.

Helene Raskin White and David Rabiner

College Drinking and Drug Use. New York: The Guilford Press, 2011.

Rin Yoshida, ed.

Trends in Alcohol Abuse and Alcoholism Research. Hauppauge, NY: Nova Science Publsihers, 2007.

Periodicals and Internet Sources

John Curran

"Vermont Latest to Eye Lower Drinking Age," *USA Today*, February 29, 2008.

Polly Curtis   "Alcohol at Home Can Cut Teenage
                            Binge Drinking, Study Says,"
                            Society-Guardian (UK), May 11,
                            2007.

Angela Fertig and   "Minimum Drinking Age Laws and
Tara Watson   Infant Health Outcomes," *Journal of
                           Health Ecomomics*, May 2009.

Kim Fromme,   "Turning 21 and the Associated
Reagan Wetherill,   Changes in Drinking and Driving
and Dan Neal   After Drinking Among College
                           Students," *Journal of American College
                           Health*, July–August 2010.

Malcolm Gladwell   "Drinking Games," *The New Yorker*,
                           February 15, 2010.

M. Alex Johnson   "Debate on Lower Drinking Age
                           Bubbling Up," MSNBC.com, August
                           14, 2007. www.msnbc.com.

Robert Kaestner   "Long-Term Effects of Minimum
and Benjamin   Legal Drinking Age Laws on Adult
Yarnoff   Alcohol Use and Driving Fatalities,"
                           Journal of Law and Economics, May
                           2011.

Michael   "The Fatal Toll of Driving to Drink:
Lovenheim and   The Effect of Minimum Legal
Joel Slemrod   Drinking Age Evasion on Traffic
                           Fatalities," *Journal of Health
                           Economics*, January 2010.

Jessica Miller   "Alcohol Most Used Drug in Utah,"
                           Standard-Examiner (Ogden, UT),
                           January 31, 2011.

John Miller   "The Case Against 21," *National
                           Review*, April 19, 2007. www.national
                           review.com.

Iain O'Neil   "Teenagers Who Drink with Their
                           Parents Are Less Likely to Binge
                           Drink, According to a Study of
                           10,000 Children," *Morning Advertiser*
                           (UK), May 11, 2007. www.morning
                           advertiser.co.uk.

Jawaid Rasul,   "Heavy Episodic Drinking on College
Robert Rommel,   Campuses: Does Changing the Legal
Geoffrey Jacquez,   Drinking Age Make a Difference?"
and Ben   *Journal of Studies on Alcohol and
Fitzpatrick   Drugs*, April 13, 2011.

Andrew M. Seder   "Alcohol Abuse Help Calls Urged,"
                           Times Leader (Wilkes-Barre, PA),
                           February 15, 2011.

Henry Wechsler   "Will Increasing Alcohol Availability
and Toben Nelson   by Lowering the Minimum Legal
                           Drinking Age Decrease Drinking and
                           Related Consequences Among
                           Youths?" *American Journal of Public
                           Health*, June 2010.

Andrew   "Alcohol at Home Could Help Cut
Woodcock   Teenage Binge Drinking," *Scotsman*
                           (UK), May 12, 2007.

Ning Zhang and   "Alcohol Policy, Social Context, and
Eric Caine   Infant Health: The Impact of
                           Minimum Legal Drinking Age,"
                           *International Journal of
                           Environmental Research and Public
                           Health*, September 23, 2011.

Index